Hibernate

*A Developer's
Notebook*™

Hibernate

A Developer's Notebook™

James Elliott

O'REILLY®

Beijing · Cambridge · Farnham · Köln · Sebastopol · Tokyo

Hibernate: A Developer's Notebook™
by James Elliott

Published by O'Reilly Media, Inc., 1005 Gravenstein Highway North, Sebastopol, CA 95472.

O'Reilly Media, Inc. books may be purchased for educational, business, or sales promotional use. Online editions are also available for most titles (*safari.oreilly.com*). For more information, contact our corporate/institutional sales department: (800) 998-9938 or *corporate@oreilly.com*.

Editor:	Mike Loukides
Production Editor:	Colleen Gorman
Cover Designer:	Edie Freedman
Interior Designer:	David Futato

Printing History:

May 2004:	First Edition.

ISBN: 978-0-596-00696-9
[M]

Contents

Preface

Hibernate is a lightweight object/relational mapping service for Java. What does that mean? It's a way to easily and efficiently work with information from a relational database in the form of natural Java objects. But that description doesn't come close to conveying how useful and exciting the technology is. I'm not the only person who thinks so: Hibernate 2.1 just won *Software Development* magazine's 14th annual Jolt Award in the "Libraries, Frameworks, and Components" category.

So, what's great about Hibernate? Every nontrivial application (and even many trivial ones) needs to store and use information, and these days this usually involves a relational database. Databases are a very different world than Java objects, and they often involve people with different skills and specializations. Bridging between the two worlds has been important for a while, but it used to be quite complex and tedious.

Most people start out struggling to write a few SQL queries, embedding these awkwardly as strings within Java code, and working with JDBC to run them and process the results. JDBC has evolved into a rich and flexible database communication library, which now provides ways to simplify and improve on this approach, but there is still a fair degree of tedium involved. People who work with data a great deal need more power, some way of moving the queries out of the code, and making them act more like well-behaved components in an object-oriented world.

Such capabilities have been part of my own (even more) lightweight object/relational layer for years. It began with a Java database connection and query pooling system written by my colleague Eric Knapp for the Lands' End e-commerce site. Our pooler introduced the idea of external SQL templates that could be accessed by name and efficiently combined with runtime data to generate the actual database queries. Only later did it grow to include the ability to bind these templates directly to Java objects, by adding simple mapping directives to the templates.

Although far less powerful than a system like Hibernate, this approach proved valuable in many projects of different sizes and in widely differing environments. I've continued to use it to this day, most recently in building IP telephony applications for Cisco's CallManager platform. But I'm going to be using Hibernate instead from now on. Once you work through this book, you'll understand why, and will probably make the same decision yourself. Hibernate does a tremendous amount for you, and does it so easily that you can almost forget you're working with a database. Your objects are simply there when you need them. This is how technology should work.

You may wonder how Hibernate relates to Enterprise JavaBeans™. Is it a competing solution? When would you use one over the other? In fact, you can use both. Most applications have no need for the complexity of EJBs, and they can simply use Hibernate directly to interact with a database. On the other hand, EJBs are indispensable for very complex three-tier application environments. In such cases, Hibernate may be used by an EJB Session bean to persist data, or it might be used to persist BMP entity beans.

How to Use This Book

The Developer's Notebook™ series is a new approach to helping readers rapidly come up to speed with useful new technologies. This book is not intended to be a comprehensive reference manual for Hibernate. Instead, it reflects my own exploration of the system, from initial download and configuration through a series of projects that demonstrate how to accomplish a variety of practical goals.

By reading and following along with these examples, you'll be able to get your own Hibernate environment set up quickly and start using it for realistic tasks right away. It's as if you can "walk with me" through terrain I've mapped out, while I point out useful landmarks and tricky pitfalls along the way.

Although I certainly include some background materials and explanations of how Hibernate works and why, this is always in the service of a focused task. Sometimes I'll refer you to the reference documentation or other online resources if you'd like more depth about one of the underlying concepts or details about a related but different way to use Hibernate.

Once you're past the first few chapters, you don't need to read the rest in order; you can jump to topics that are particularly interesting or relevant to you. The examples do build on each other, but you can download the finished source code from the book's web site (you may want to start with the previous chapter's files and follow along making changes yourself to implement the examples you're reading). You can always jump back to the earlier examples if they turn out to be interesting because of how they relate to what you've just learned.

Font Conventions

This book follows certain conventions for font usage. Understanding these conventions up-front makes it easier to use this book.

Italic

Used for filenames, file extensions, URLs, application names, emphasis, and new terms when they are first introduced.

`Constant width`

Used for Java class names, methods, variables, properties, data types, database elements, and snippets of code that appear in text.

`Constant width bold`

Used for commands you enter at the command line and to highlight new code inserted in a running example.

`Constant width italic`

Used to annotate output.

On the Web Site

The web site for this book, *http://www.oreilly.com/catalog/0596006969*, offers some important materials you'll want to know about. All the examples for this book can be found there, organized by chapter.

The examples are available as a ZIP archive and a compressed TAR archive.

In many cases, the same files are used throughout a series of chapters, and they evolve to include new features and capabilities from example to example. Each chapter folder in the downloadable archive contains a snapshot of the state of the example system, reflecting all the changes and new content introduced in that chapter.

How to Contact Us

Please address comments and questions concerning this book to the publisher:

O'Reilly & Associates, Inc.
1005 Gravenstein Highway North
Sebastopol, CA 95472
(800) 998-9938 (in the United States or Canada)
(707) 829-0515 (international or local)
(707) 829-0104 (fax)

O'Reilly's web page for this book, where we list errata, examples, or any additional information. You can access this page at:

http://www.oreilly.com/catalog/hibernate/

To comment or ask technical questions about this book, send email to:

bookquestions@oreilly.com

For more information about our books, conferences, Resource Centers, and the O'Reilly Network, see our web site at:

http://www.oreilly.com/

Acknowledgments

Any list of thanks has to start with my parents for fostering my interest in computing even when we were living in countries that made that a major challenge, and with my partner Joe for putting up with it today when it has flowered into a major obsession. I'd also like to acknowledge my employer, Berbee, for giving me an opportunity to delve deeply into Java and build skills as an architect of reusable APIs; for letting me stay clear of the proprietary, platform-specific tar pit that is engulfing so much of the programming world; for surrounding me with such incredible colleagues; and for being supportive when I wanted to leverage these experiences in writing this book.

Marc Loy got me connected with the wonderful folks at O'Reilly by inviting me to help with the second edition of *Java Swing*, and Mike Loukides has been patiently working on me ever since—encouraging me to write a book of my own. In Hibernate he found the perfect topic to get me started. Deb Cameron, our revisions editor for the *Swing* effort, has played a big role in turning my tentative authorial ambitions into a rewarding reality. I'm also grateful she was willing to "loan me out" from helping with the third edition of *Learning Emacs* to take on the Hibernate project.

I'm particularly indebted to my technical reviewers: Adrian Kellor and Curt Pederson. They looked at some very early drafts and helped set my tone and direction, as well as reinforcing my enthusiasm about the value of this project. As the book came together, Bruce Tate provided an important sanity check from someone actively using and teaching Hibernate, and he offered some great advice and even more encouragement. Eric Knapp reviewed a large portion with an eye toward using the book in an instructional setting at a technical college, and reminded me to keep my feet on the ground. Tim Cartwright jumped in at the end, working with a nearly complete draft in an effort to understand Hibernate as a potential platform for future work, and providing a great deal of useful feedback about the content and presentation.

I'd also like to thank the many members of O'Reilly's production department who put in lots of work under an unusually tight schedule.

## CHAPTER 1

Installation and Setup

It continues to amaze me how many great, free, open source Java™ tools are out there. When I needed a lightweight object/relational mapping service for a JSP e-commerce project several years ago, I had to build my own. It evolved over the years, developed some cool and unique features, and we've used it in a wide variety of different contexts. But now that I've discovered Hibernate, I expect that I'll be using it on my next project instead of my own familiar system (toward which I'll cheerfully admit bias). That should tell you how compelling it is!

Since you're looking at this book, you're interested in a powerful and convenient way to bridge between the worlds of Java objects and relational databases. Hibernate fills that role very nicely, without being so big and complicated that learning it becomes a daunting challenge in itself. To demonstrate that, this chapter guides you to the point where you can play with Hibernate and see for yourself why it's so exciting.

Getting an Ant Distribution

If you're not already using Ant to manage the building, testing, running, and packaging of your Java projects, now is the time to start. The examples in this book are Ant driven, so you'll need a working Ant installation to follow along and experiment with variations on your own system, which is the best way to learn.

First of all, get an Ant binary and install it.

Why do I care?

We chose to structure our examples around Ant for several reasons. It's convenient and powerful, it's increasingly (almost universally) the standard build tool for Java-based development, it's free and it's cross-platform. Many of the example and helper scripts in the current Hibernate distribution are Windows batch files, which don't do any good for people like me who live in a Unix world. Using Ant means our examples can work equally well anywhere there's a Java environment, which means we don't have to frustrate or annoy any readers of this book. Happily, it also means we can do many more cool things with less effort—especially since several Hibernate tools have explicit Ant support, which we'll show how to leverage.

To take advantage of all this, you need to have Ant installed and working on your system.

How do I do that?

Download a binary release of Ant from *http://ant.apache.org/bindownload.cgi*. Scroll down to find the current release of Ant, and download the archive in a format that's convenient for you to work with. Pick an appropriate place for it to live, and expand the archive there. The directory into which you've expanded the archive is referred to as ANT_HOME. Let's say you've expanded the archive into the directory */usr/local/apache-ant-1.5.1*; you may want to create a symbolic link to make it easier to work with, and to avoid the need to change any environment configuration when you upgrade to a newer version:

```
/usr/local $ ln -s apache-ant-1.5.1 ant
```

Once Ant is situated, you need to do a couple of things to make it work right. You need to add its *bin* directory in the distribution (in our example, */usr/local/ant/bin*) to your command path. You also need to set the environment variable ANT_HOME to the top-level directory you installed (in this example, */usr/local/ant*). Details about how to perform these steps under different operating systems can be found in the Ant manual, *http://ant.apache.org/manual/*, if you need them.

Of course, we're also assuming you've got a Java SDK. Because some of Hibernate's features are available only in Java 1.4, you'd be best off upgrading to the latest 1.4 SDK. It's also possible to use most of Hibernate with Java 1.3, but you may have to rebuild the Hibernate JAR file using your 1.3 compiler. Our examples are written assuming you've got Java 1.4, and they will need tweaking if you don't.

Once you've got this set up, you should be able to fire up Ant for a test run and verify that everything's right:

```
~ $ ant -version
Apache Ant version 1.5.1 compiled on February 7 2003
```

What just happened?

Well, not much just yet, but you're now in a position where you'll be able to try out the examples we provide later on, and use them as a starting point for your actual Hibernate projects.

If you're new to Ant, it wouldn't be a bad idea to read the manual a little bit to get a sense of how it works and what it can do for you; this will help make sense of the *build.xml* files we start working with in our examples. If you decide (or already know) you like Ant, and want to dig deeper, you can pick up O'Reilly's *Ant: The Definitive Guide* (after you finish *this* book, of course)!

What about...

...Eclipse, JBuilder, Sun ONE Studio (Forte for Java), or some other Java IDE? Well, you can certainly use these, but you're on your own as far as what you need to do to get Ant integrated into the build process. (Several already use Ant, so you might be starting out ahead; for the others you might have to jump through some hoops.) If all else fails, you can use the IDE to develop your own code, but invoke Ant from the command line when you need to use one of our build scripts.

Getting the HSQLDB Database Engine

Hibernate works with a great many relational databases; chances are, it will work with the one you are planning to use for your next project. We need to pick one to focus on in our examples, and luckily there's an obvious choice. The free, open source, 100% Java HSQLDB project is powerful enough that it forms the backing storage for several of our commercial software projects. Surprisingly, it's also incredibly self-contained and simple to install, so it's perfect to discuss here. (If you've heard of HypersonicSQL, this is its current incarnation. Much of the Hibernate documentation uses the older name.)

TIP

Don't panic if you end up at *http://hsql.sourceforge.net/* and it seems like the project has been shut down. That's the wrong address—it's talking about the predecessor to the current HSQLDB project. Use the address below to find the current version of the database engine.

Why do I care?

Examples based on a database that everyone can download and easily experiment with mean you won't have to translate any of the SQL dialects or operating system commands to work with your available databases (and may even mean you can save a day or two learning how to download, install, and configure one of the more typical database environments). Finally, if hsqldb is new to you, chances are good you'll be impressed and intrigued, and may well end up using it in your own projects. As it says on the project home page (at *http://hsqldb.sourceforge.net*):

> hsqldb is a relational database engine written in Java, with a JDBC driver, supporting a rich subset of ANSI-92 SQL (BNF tree format). It offers a small (less than 160k), fast database engine which offers both in memory and disk based tables. Embedded and server modes are available. Additionally, it includes tools such as a minimal web server, in-memory query and management tools (can be run as applets), and a number of demonstration examples.

Go on, download HSQLDB. Heck, take two, they're small!

How do I do that?

Getting the database is simply a matter of visiting the project page at *http://hsqldb.sourceforge.net* and clicking the link to download the current stable version. This will take you to a typical SourceForge downloads page with the current release highlighted. Pick your mirror and download the zip archive. There's nothing to install or configure; we'll show you how to use it shortly.

What about...

...MySQL, PostgreSQL, Oracle, DB2, Sybase, Informix, or some other common database? Don't worry, Hibernate can work with all these and others. We'll talk about how you specify "dialects" for different databases later on. And if you really want, you can try to figure out how to work with your favorite from the start, but it will mean extra work for you in following along with the examples, and you'll miss out on a great opportunity to discover HSQLDB.

Getting Hibernate

This doesn't need much motivation! You picked up this book because you wanted to learn how to use Hibernate.

How do I do that?

Go to the Hibernate home page, *http://www.hibernate.org/*, and click on the "Download" link. The Binary Releases section will tell you which version is recommended for downloading; follow that advice. Make a note of the version you want and proceed to the "Download: SourceForge" link. It takes you to a SourceForge downloads page. Scroll down until you find the recommended release version of Hibernate itself (which will look something like *hibernate-2.x.y.zip* or *hibernate-2.x.y.tar.gz*). Choose the archive format that is most convenient for you and download it.

Pick a place that is suitable for keeping such items around, and expand the archive. We will use part of it in the next step, and investigate more of it later on. You may also want to poke around in there some yourself.

While you're on the Hibernate downloads page, also pick up the Hibernate Extensions. They contain several useful tools which aren't necessary for an application running Hibernate, but are very helpful for developers creating such applications. We'll be using one to generate Java code for our first Hibernate experiment in the next chapter. This filename will look like *hibernate-extensions-2.x.y.zip* (it won't necessarily have the same version as Hibernate itself). Once again, pick your favorite archive format, download this file, and expand it next to where you put Hibernate.

Setting Up a Project Hierarchy

Although we're going to start small, once we start designing data structures and building Java classes and database tables that represent them, along with all the configuration and control files to glue them together and make useful things happen, we're going to end up with a lot of files. So let's start out with a good organization from the beginning. As you'll see in this process, between the tools you've downloaded and their supporting libraries, there are already a significant number of files to organize.

Why do I care?

If you end up building something cool by following the examples in this book, and want to turn it into a real application, you'll be in good shape from the beginning. More to the point, if you set things up the way we describe here, the commands and instructions we give you throughout the examples will make sense and actually work. Many examples also build on one another throughout the book, so it's important to get on the right track from the beginning.

If you want to skip ahead to a later example, or just avoid typing some of the longer sample code and configuration files, you can download "finished" versions of the chapter examples from the book's web site. These downloads will all be organized as described here.

How do I do that?

Here's how:

1. Pick a location on your hard drive where you want to play with Hibernate, and create a new folder, which we'll refer to from now on as your *project directory*.

2. Move into that directory, and create subdirectories called *src*, *lib*, and *data*. The hierarchy of Java source and related resources will be in the *src* directory. Our build process will compile it into a *classes* directory it creates, as well as copy any runtime resources there. The *data* directory is where we'll put the HSQLDB database, and any Data Definition Language (DDL) files we generate in order to populate it.

   The *lib* directory is where we'll place third-party libraries we use in the project. For now, copy the HSQLDB and Hibernate JAR files into the *lib* directory.

3. If you haven't already done so, expand the HSQLDB distribution file you downloaded earlier in this chapter. You'll find *hsqldb.jar* in its *lib* directory; copy this to your own project *lib* directory (the *lib* directory you just created in step 2).

4. Similarly, locate the *lib* directory in the Hibernate directory you expanded in the previous section, and copy all of its contents into your own project *lib* directory (you'll notice that Hibernate relies on a lot of other libraries; conveniently, they're included in its binary distribution so you don't have to hunt them all down yourself).

5. Then copy Hibernate itself, in the form of the *hibernate2.jar* file found at the top level of the distribution, into your project *lib* directory.

6. Installing the Hibernate Extensions is very similar. Locate the *tools/lib* directory inside the Hibernate Extensions directory you expanded, and copy its contents into your own *lib* directory, so the extensions will be able to access the libraries they rely on.

7. Finally, copy the extensions themselves, which are in the file *hibernate-tools.jar* (found in the *tools* directory), into your *lib* directory.

8. The example classes we're going to create are all going to live in the com.oreilly.hh (harnessing Hibernate) package, so create these directories under the *src* directory. On Linux and Mac OS X, you can use:

```
mkdir -p src/com/oreilly/hh
```

from within your project directory to accomplish this in one step.

There are lots of pieces to copy into place here; attention to detail will be rewarded. Luckily, you can reuse your lib directory in other Hibernate projects.

At this point your project directory should be structured as shown in Figure 1-1.

Figure 1-1. Initial project directory contents

The *lib* directory is collapsed because it contains so much that the screen shot wouldn't fit otherwise. After following the above steps, using the release of Hibernate available at the time of this writing, it contains the following files:

README.txt, ant-1.5.3.jar, ant-optional-1.5.3.jar, apache.license.txt, c3p0-0.8.3.jar, c3p0.license.txt, cglib-2.0-rc2.jar, commons-collections-2.1.jar, commons-dbcp-1.1.jar, commons-lang-1.0.1.jar, commons-logging-1.0.3.jar, commons-pool-1.1.jar, concurrent-1.3.2.jar, connector.jar, connector.licence.txt, dom4j-1.4.jar, ehcache-0.6.jar, hibernate-tools.jar, hibernate2.jar, hsqldb.jar, jaas.jar, jaas.licence.txt, jboss-cache.jar, jboss-common.jar, jboss-jmx.jar, jboss-system.jar, jcs-1.0-dev.jar, jdbc2_0-stdext.jar, jdbc2_0-stdext.licence.txt, jdom.jar, jdom.license.txt, jgroups-2.2.jar, jta.jar, jta.licence.txt, junit-3.8.1.jar, log4j-1.2.8.jar, odmg-3.0.jar, oscache-2.0.jar, proxool-0.8.3.jar, swarmcache-1.0rc2.jar, xalan-2.4.0.jar, xerces-2.4.0.jar, xml-apis.jar.

A quick test

Before we get into actually rousing Hibernate to do some useful work, it's worth checking that the other supporting pieces are in place and ready to use. Let's start out with the Ant configuration file we'll be using throughout this project, tell Ant where we've put the files we're using, and have it fire up the HSQLDB graphical database interface. This will be useful later when we want to look at the actual data that Hibernate has been creating for us, and it's reassuring right now as a sanity check that nothing is amiss and we're ready to move forward.

Fire up your favorite text editor and create a file named *build.xml* at the top level inside your project directory (the folder *ch01* in Figure 1-1). Type the content shown in Example 1-1 into the file.

Example 1-1. Ant build file

```
1   <?xml version="1.0"?>
2   <project name="Harnessing Hibernate: The Developer's Notebook"
3           default="db" basedir=".">
4     <!-- Set up properties containing important project directories -->
5     <property name="source.root" value="src"/>
6     <property name="class.root" value="classes"/>
7     <property name="lib.dir" value="lib"/>
8     <property name="data.dir" value="data"/>
9
10    <!-- Set up the class path for compilation and execution -->
11    <path id="project.class.path">
12        <!-- Include our own classes, of course -->
13        <pathelement location="${class.root}"/>
14        <!-- Include jars in the project library directory -->
15        <fileset dir="${lib.dir}">
16          <include name="**/*.jar"/>
17        </fileset>
18    </path>
19
20    <target name="db" description="Runs HSQLDB database management UI
21  against the database file--use when application is not running">
22        <java classname="org.hsqldb.util.DatabaseManager"
23            fork="yes">
24          <classpath refid="project.class.path"/>
25          <arg value="-driver"/>
26          <arg value="org.hsqldb.jdbcDriver"/>
27          <arg value="-url"/>
28          <arg value="jdbc:hsqldb:${data.dir}/music"/>
29          <arg value="-user"/>
30          <arg value="sa"/>
31        </java>
32    </target>
33  </project>
```

If you haven't seen an Ant build file before, here's a whirlwind introduction to help orient you. The documentation at *http://ant.apache.org/manual/index.html* is quite good if you want a bit more detail. The first line is simply a declaration that the type of the file is XML. If you've worked with XML in other contexts, you're used to seeing this. If not, you'll see it again. (Ant doesn't currently require this, but most XML parsers do, so it's a good habit to develop.)

Ant's build files always contain a single `project` definition, which begins in this file on line 2. The `default` attribute tells Ant which *target* (defined below) to build if you don't specify any on the command line. And the `basedir` attribute determines the "directory relative to which all path calculations are done. We could have left this out since the default is to treat paths as being relative to the directory in which the *build.xml* is located, but it's a good habit to be explicit about fundamental settings.

The next bit, starting at line 4, defines four *properties* that we can use by name throughout the rest of the build file. Essentially, we're defining symbolic names for the important directories used for different aspects of the project. This isn't necessary (especially when the directories are named so simply), but it's another good practice. For one thing, it means that if you need to change where one of these directories is located, you only need to fix one place in the build file, rather than conducting an error-prone search-and-replace.

The class path section starting at line 10 serves a more obviously useful purpose. This feature alone is why I almost never start Java projects without setting up at least a simple Ant build for them. When you're using a lot of third-party libraries, which you're going to be doing for any serious project, there's a whole lot that needs to go into your class path, and you have to be sure to set it equivalently at compile time and runtime. Ant makes this very easy. We define a *path*, which is kind of like a property, but it knows how to parse and collect files and directories. Our path contains the *classes* directory, in which we're going to be compiling our Java source (this directory doesn't exist yet; we'll add a step to the build process that creates it in the next chapter), and it also contains all JAR files that can be found in our library directory. This is exactly what we need for compiling and running.

The syntax on line 13 looks like punctuation soup, but it can be broken down into pieces that make sense. Ant lets you use *substitution* to insert variable values into your rules. Where you see something like "${class.root}" this means "look up the value of the variable named class.root and stick it here." So, given the definition of class.root on line 6, it's as if line 12 contained "<pathelement location="classes"/>". So why do this? It lets you share a value throughout the file, so if you ever need to change it there's only one place to worry about. In large, complex projects this kind of organization and management is crucial.

Finally, with all this preamble out of the way we can define our first target at line 20. A target is just a series of *tasks* that need to be executed in order to accomplish a project goal. Typical targets do things like compile code, run tests, package things up for distribution, and the like. Tasks are chosen from a rich set of capabilities built-in to Ant, and third-party tools like Hibernate can extend Ant to provide their own useful tasks, as we'll see in the next chapter. Our first target, db, is going to run HSQLDB's graphical interface so we can look at our example database. We can accomplish that using Ant's built-in java task, which runs a Java virtual machine for us, with whatever starting class, arguments, and properties we'd like.

In this case, the class we want to invoke is org.hsqldb.util. DatabaseManager, found in *hsqldb.jar* in our project library directory. Setting the fork attribute to "yes" tells Ant to use a separate virtual machine, which isn't the default since it takes a little longer and isn't usually necessary. In this case it's important since we want the database manager GUI to stay around until we dismiss it, and this doesn't happen when it runs in Ant's own VM.

You can see how we're telling the java task about the class path we've set up above; this will be a common feature of our targets. Then we supply a bunch of arguments to the database manager, telling it to use the normal HSQLDB JDBC driver, where to find the database, and what username to use. We've specified a database called "music" in the *data* directory. That directory is currently empty, so HSQLDB will create the database the first time we use it. The user sa is the default "system administrator" user for new databases, and it's configured not to need a password initially. Obviously, if you plan to make this database available over the network (which HSQLDB is capable of doing) you'll want to set a password. We aren't doing any such fancy things, so we can leave it out for now.

Let's try it! Save the file and from a shell (command) prompt running in your top-level project directory (where you put *build.xml*) type the command:

```
ant db
```

(or, since we've made db the default target, you can just type **ant**). Once Ant starts running, if all goes well, you'll see output like this:

```
Buildfile: build.xml

db:
```

A moment later you should see the HSQLDB graphic interface, which will look something like Figure 1-2. There's nothing in our database yet, so there's not much to see beyond whether the command worked at all. The tree view at the top left of the window is where the various tables and columns in our database can be explored. For now, just verify that the top reads "jdbc:hsqldb:data/music." You can explore the menus a bit if you like, but don't make any changes to the database. Once you're done, choose File → Exit. The window will close, and Ant will report:

```
BUILD SUCCESSFUL
Total time: 18 minutes 3 seconds
```

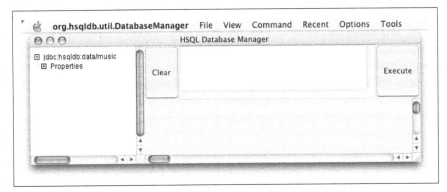

Figure 1-2. The HSQLDB database manager interface

The "Total time" reflects how long you were running the database manager, so it will vary. At this point, if you look in the data directory, you'll find that HSQLDB has created some files to hold the database:

```
music.properties music.script
```

You can even look at the contents of these files. Unlike most database systems, HSQLDB stores its data in a human-readable format. The properties file contains some basic settings, and the data itself goes in the script file in the form of SQL statements. Right now all you'll find is the basic definitions that get entered by default, but as later examples start populating the database, you'll be able to see DDL and SQL statements that

The fact that you can read HSQLDB's database files is weird but fun.

create the tables and data. This can be a useful debugging feature for basic sanity checks, even faster than firing up the graphical interface and running queries.

What just happened?

Well, to be honest, you jumped through a lot of hoops to find, download, expand, and organize a bunch of software. It was probably pretty tedious and exacting. But you're now in a great position to start working with Hibernate and, as you'll see in the next chapter, that means progress will start happening very quickly. You'll be able to see Java code written for you! Database schemas created out of thin air (or, at least, out of the same XML mapping table that produced the Java)! Real tables and data appearing in the HSQLDB manager interface! (Or, at least, genuine faux sample data....)

Sound exciting? Well, compared to what you've done so far anyway? Then let's dig in to awakening the power of Hibernate.

Why didn't it work?

If, on the other hand, you saw no database manager window appear, and instead were greeted by error messages, try to figure out if they're due to problems in the build file, problems in the way you've set up Ant or your project hierarchy, or something else. Double-check that all the pieces are arranged and installed as shown earlier, and consider downloading the sample code if you are having trouble with a version you typed in yourself.

## CHAPTER 2

Introduction to Mapping

Now that we're in a position to work with Hibernate, it's worth pausing to reflect on why we wanted to in the first place, lest we remain lost in the details of installation and configuration. Object-oriented languages like Java provide a powerful and convenient abstraction for working with information at runtime in the form of objects that instantiate classes. These objects can link up with each other in a myriad of ways, and they can embody rules and behavior as well as the raw data they represent. But when the program ends, all the objects swiftly and silently vanish.

For information we need to keep around between runs, or share between different programs and systems, relational databases have proven to be hard to beat. They're scalable, reliable, efficient, and extremely flexible. So what we need is a means of taking information from a SQL database and turning it into Java objects, and vice versa.

There are many different ways of doing this, ranging from completely manual database design and coding, to highly automated tools. The general problem is known as Object/Relational Mapping, and Hibernate is a lightweight O/R mapping service for Java.

The "lightweight" designation means it is designed to be fairly simple to learn and use, and to place reasonable demands on system resources, compared to some of the other available tools. Despite this, it manages to be broadly useful and deep. The designers have done a good job of figuring out the kinds of things that real projects need to accomplish, and supporting them well.

You can use Hibernate in many different ways, depending on what you're starting with. If you've got a database that you need to interact with, there are tools that can analyze the existing schema as a starting point for your mapping, and help you write the Java classes to represent

In this chapter:
- *Writing a Mapping Document*
- *Generating Some Class*
- *Cooking Up a Schema*
- *Connecting Hibernate to MySQL*

the data. If you've got classes that you want to store in a new database, you can start with the classes, get help building a mapping document, and generate an initial database schema. We'll look at some of these approaches later.

For now, we're going to see how you can start a brand new project, with no existing classes or data, and have Hibernate help you build both. When starting from scratch like this, the most convenient place to begin is in the middle, with an abstract definition of the mapping we're going to make between program objects and the database tables that will store them.

In our examples we're going to be working with a database that could power an interface to a large personal collection of music, allowing users to search, browse, and listen in a natural way. (You might well have guessed this from the names of the database files that were created at the end of the first chapter.)

Writing a Mapping Document

Hibernate uses an XML document to track the mapping between Java classes and relational database tables. This *mapping document* is designed to be readable and hand-editable. You can also start by using graphical CASE tools (like Together, Rose, or Poseidon) to build UML diagrams representing your data model, and feed these into AndroMDA (*http://www.andromda.org/*), turning them into Hibernate mappings.

Don't forget that Hibernate and its extensions let you work in other ways, starting with classes or data if you've got them.

We'll write one by hand, showing it's quite practical.

We're going to start by writing a mapping document for *tracks*, pieces of music that can be listened to individually or as part of an album or play list. To begin with, we'll keep track of the track's title, the path to the file containing the actual music, its playing time, the date on which it was added to the database, and the volume at which it should be played (in case the default volume isn't appropriate because it was recorded at a very different level than other music in the database).

Why do I care?

You might not have any need for a new system to keep track of your music, but the concepts and process involved in setting up this mapping will translate to the projects you actually want to tackle.

How do I do that?

Fire up your favorite text editor, and create the file *Track.hbm.xml* in the *src/com/oreilly/hh* directory you set up in the previous chapter. (If you skipped that chapter, you'll need to go back and follow it, because this example relies on the project structure and tools we set up there.) Type in the mapping document as shown in Example 2-1. Or, if you'd rather avoid all that typing, download the code examples from this book's web site, and find the mapping file in the directory for Chapter 2.

Example 2-1. The mapping document for tracks, *Track.hbm.xml*

```
 1  <?xml version="1.0"?>
 2  <!DOCTYPE hibernate-mapping
 3          PUBLIC "-//Hibernate/Hibernate Mapping DTD 2.0//EN"
 4          "http://hibernate.sourceforge.net/hibernate-mapping-2.0.dtd">
 5  <hibernate-mapping>
 6
 7    <class name="com.oreilly.hh.Track" table="TRACK">
 8      <meta attribute="class-description">
 9        Represents a single playable track in the music database.
10        @author Jim Elliott (with help from Hibernate)
11      </meta>
12
13      <id name="id" type="int" column="TRACK_ID">
14        <meta attribute="scope-set">protected</meta>
15        <generator class="native"/>
16      </id>
17
18      <property name="title" type="string" not-null="true"/>
19
20      <property name="filePath" type="string" not-null="true"/>
21
22      <property name="playTime" type="time">
23        <meta attribute="field-description">Playing time</meta>
24      </property>
25
26      <property name="added" type="date">
27        <meta attribute="field-description">When the track was created</meta>
28      </property>
29
30      <property name="volume" type="short">
31        <meta attribute="field-description">How loud to play the track</meta>
32      </property>
33
34    </class>
35  </hibernate-mapping>
```

The first four lines are a required preamble to make this a valid XML document and announce that it conforms to the document type definition used by Hibernate for mappings. The actual mappings are inside the hibernate-mapping tag. Starting at line 7 we're defining a mapping for a single class, com.oreilly.hh.Track, and the name and package of this class are related to the name and location of the file we've created. This relationship isn't necessary; you can define mappings for any number of classes in a single mapping document, and name it and locate it anywhere you want, as long as you tell Hibernate how to find it. The advantage of following the convention of naming the mapping file after the class it maps, and placing it in the same place on the class path as that class, is that this allows Hibernate to automatically locate the mapping when you want to work with the class. This simplifies the configuration and use of Hibernate.

In the opening of the class tag on line 7, we have also specified that this class is stored in a database table named TRACK. The next tag, a meta tag (lines 8–11), doesn't directly affect the mapping. Instead, it provides additional information that can be used by different tools. In this case, by specifying an attribute value of "class-description," we are telling the Java code generation tool the JavaDoc text we want associated with the Track class. This is entirely optional, and you'll see the result of including it in the upcoming section, "Generating Some Class."

TIP

Although databases vary in terms of whether they keep track of the capitalization of table and column names, this book will use the convention of referring to these database entities in all-caps, to help clarify when something being discussed is a database column or table, as opposed to a persistent Java class or property.

The remainder of the mapping sets up the pieces of information we want to keep track of, as properties in the class and their associated columns in the database table. Even though we didn't mention it in the introduction to this example, each track is going to need an *id*. Following database best practices, we'll use a meaningless *surrogate key* (a value with no semantic meaning, serving only to identify a specific database row). In Hibernate, the key/id mapping is set up using an id tag (starting at line 13). We're choosing to use an int to store our id in the database column TRACK_ID, which will correspond to the property id in our Track object. This mapping contains another meta tag to communicate with the Java code generator, telling it that the set method for the id property should be protected—there's no need for application code to go changing track IDs.

The generator tag on line 15 configures how Hibernate creates id values for new instances. (Note that it relates to normal O/R mapping operation, *not* to the Java code generator, which is often not even used; generator is more fundamental than the optional meta tags.) There are a number of different ID generation strategies to choose from, and you can even write your own. In this case, we're telling Hibernate to use whatever is most natural for the underlying database (we'll see later on how it learns what database we're using). In the case of HSQLDB, an identity column is used.

You may be thinking there's a lot of dense information in this file. That's true, and as you'll see, it can be used to create a bunch of useful project resources.

After the id, we just enumerate the various track properties we care about. The title (line 18) is a string, and it cannot be null. The filePath (line 20) has the same characteristics, while the remainder are allowed to be null: playTime (line 22) is a time, added (line 26) is a date, and volume (line 30) is a short. These last three properties use a new kind of meta attribute, "field-description," which specifies JavaDoc text for the individual properties, with some limitations in the current code generator.

What just happened?

We took the abstract description of the information about music tracks that we wanted to represent in our Java code and database, and turned it into a rigorous specification in the format that Hibernate can read. Hopefully you'll agree that it's a pretty compact and readable representation of the information. Next we'll look at what Hibernate can actually do with it.

What about...

...Other data types, including nested classes and enumerations? Relationships between tables? Indices? Class hierarchies and polymorphism? Tables that contain rows we need to ignore? Hibernate can handle all these things, and we'll cover most of them in later examples. Appendix A lists the basic types that Hibernate supports "out of the box."

Generating Some Class

Our mapping contains information about both the database and the Java class between which it maps. We can use it to help us create both. Let's look at the class first.

How do I do that?

The Hibernate Extensions you installed in Chapter 1 included a tool that can write Java source matching the specifications in a mapping document, and an Ant task that makes it easy to invoke from within an Ant build file. Edit *build.xml* to add the portions shown in bold in Example 2-2.

Example 2-2. The Ant build file updated for code generation

```
1   <project name="Harnessing Hibernate: The Developer's Notebook"
2          default="db" basedir=".">
3   <!-- Set up properties containing important project directories -->
4   <property name="source.root" value="src"/>
5   <property name="class.root" value="classes"/>
6   <property name="lib.dir" value="lib"/>
7   <property name="data.dir" value="data"/>
8
9   <!-- Set up the class path for compilation and execution -->
10  <path id="project.class.path">
11      <!-- Include our own classes, of course -->
12      <pathelement location="${class.root}" />
13      <!-- Include jars in the project library directory -->
14      <fileset dir="${lib.dir}">
15        <include name="*.jar"/>
16      </fileset>
17  </path>
18
19  <target name="db" description="Runs HSQLDB database management UI
20  against the database file--use when application is not running">
21      <java classname="org.hsqldb.util.DatabaseManager"
22          fork="yes">
23        <classpath refid="project.class.path"/>
24        <arg value="-driver"/>
25        <arg value="org.hsqldb.jdbcDriver"/>
26        <arg value="-url"/>
27        <arg value="jdbc:hsqldb:${data.dir}/music"/>
28        <arg value="-user"/>
29        <arg value="sa"/>
30      </java>
31  </target>
32
33  <!-- Teach Ant how to use Hibernate's code generation tool -->
34  <taskdef name="hbm2java"
35          classname="net.sf.hibernate.tool.hbm2java.Hbm2JavaTask"
36          classpathref="project.class.path"/>
37
38  <!-- Generate the java code for all mapping files in our source tree -->
39  <target name="codegen"
40          description="Generate Java source from the O/R mapping files">
41    <hbm2java output="${source.root}">
42      <fileset dir="${source.root}">
```

Example 2-2. *The Ant build file updated for code generation (continued)*

```
43              <include name="**/*.hbm.xml"/>
44          </fileset>
45        </hbm2java>
46      </target>
47
48  </project>
```

We added a `taskdef` (task definition) and a new target to the build file. The task definition at line 33 teaches Ant a new trick: it tells Ant how to use the *hbm2java* tool that is part of the Hibernate Extensions, with the help of a class provided for this purpose. Note that it also specifies the class path to be used when invoking this tool, using the `project.class.path` definition found earlier in the file.

The codegen target at line 38 uses the new `hbm2java` task to run Hibernate's code generator on any mapping documents found in the *src* tree, writing the corresponding Java source. The pattern "`**/*.hbm.xml`" means "any file ending in *.hbm.xml*, within the specified directory, or any subdirectory, however deeply nested."

Let's try it! From within your top-level project directory (the folder containing *build.xml*), type the following command:

    ant codegen

You should see output like this:

```
Buildfile: build.xml

codegen:
  [hbm2java] Processing 1 files.
  [hbm2java] Building hibernate objects
  [hbm2java] log4j:WARN No appenders could be found for logger (net.sf.
hibernate.util.DTDEntityResolver).
  [hbm2java] log4j:WARN Please initialize the log4j system properly.
```

The warnings are griping about the fact that we haven't taken the trouble to set up the logging environment that Hibernate expects. We'll see how to do that in the next example. For now, if you look in the directory *src/com/oreilly/hh*, you'll see that a new file named *Track.java* has appeared, with the content shown in Example 2-3.

Example 2-3. *Code generated from the Track mapping document*

```
1   package com.oreilly.hh;
2
3   import java.io.Serializable;
4   import java.util.Date;
5   import org.apache.commons.lang.builder.EqualsBuilder;
6   import org.apache.commons.lang.builder.HashCodeBuilder;
```

Example 2-3. *Code generated from the Track mapping document (continued)*

```
7   import org.apache.commons.lang.builder.ToStringBuilder;
8
9   /**
10   *        Represents a single playable track in the music database.
11   *        @author Jim Elliott (with help from Hibernate)
12   *
13   */
14   public class Track implements Serializable {
15
16       /** identifier field */
17       private Integer id;
18
19       /** persistent field */
20       private String title;
21
22       /** persistent field */
23       private String filePath;
24
25       /** nullable persistent field */
26       private Date playTime;
27
28       /** nullable persistent field */
29       private Date added;
30
31       /** nullable persistent field */
32       private short volume;
33
34       /** full constructor */
35       public Track(String title, String filePath, Date playTime,
                       Date added, short volume) {
36           this.title = title;
37           this.filePath = filePath;
38           this.playTime = playTime;
39           this.added = added;
40           this.volume = volume;
41       }
42
43       /** default constructor */
44       public Track() {
45       }
46
47       /** minimal constructor */
48       public Track(String title, String filePath) {
49           this.title = title;
50           this.filePath = filePath;
51       }
52
53       public Integer getId() {
54           return this.id;
55       }
56
57       protected void setId(Integer id) {
```

Example 2-3. Code generated from the Track mapping document (continued)

```
58          this.id = id;
59      }
60
61      public String getTitle() {
62          return this.title;
63      }
64
65      public void setTitle(String title) {
66          this.title = title;
67      }
68
69      public String getFilePath() {
70          return this.filePath;
71      }
72
73      public void setFilePath(String filePath) {
74          this.filePath = filePath;
75      }
76
77      /**
78       * Playing time
79       */
80      public Date getPlayTime() {
81          return this.playTime;
82      }
83
84      public void setPlayTime(Date playTime) {
85          this.playTime = playTime;
86      }
87
88      /**
89       * When the track was created
90       */
91      public Date getAdded() {
92          return this.added;
93      }
94
95      public void setAdded(Date added) {
96          this.added = added;
97      }
98
99      /**
100      * How loud to play the track
101      */
102     public short getVolume() {
103         return this.volume;
104     }
105
106     public void setVolume(short volume) {
107         this.volume = volume;
108     }
109
```

Example 2-3. Code generated from the Track mapping document (continued)

```
110     public String toString() {
111         return new ToStringBuilder(this)
112             .append("id", getId())
113             .toString();
114     }
115
116     public boolean equals(Object other) {
117         if ( !(other instanceof Track) ) return false;
118         Track castOther = (Track) other;
119         return new EqualsBuilder()
120             .append(this.getId(), castOther.getId())
121             .isEquals();
122     }
123
124     public int hashCode() {
125         return new HashCodeBuilder()
126             .append(getId())
127             .toHashCode();
128     }
129
130 }
```

What just happened?

Ant found all files in our source tree ending in *.hbm.xml* (just one, so far) and fed it to the Hibernate code generator, which analyzed it, and wrote a Java class meeting the specifications we provided for the Track mapping.

That can save a lot of time and fairly repetitive activity. I could get used to it.

You may find it worthwhile to compare the generated Java source with the mapping specification from which it arose (Example 2-1). The source starts out with the proper package declaration, which is easy for *hbm2java* to figure out from the fully qualified class name required in the mapping file. There are a couple of imports to make the source more readable. The three potentially unfamiliar entries (lines 5–7) are utilities from the Jakarta Commons project that help in the creation of correctly implemented and useful toString(), equals(), and hashCode() methods.

The class-level JavaDoc at line 10 should look familiar, since it comes right from the "class-description" meta tag in our mapping document. The field declarations are derived from the id (line 17) and property (lines 20–32) tags defined in the mapping. The Java types used are derived from the property types in the mapping document. We'll delve into the full set of value types supported by Hibernate later on. For now, the relationship between the types in the mapping document and the Java types used in the generated code should be fairly clear.

One curious detail is that an Integer wrapper has been used for id, while volume is declared as a simple, unwrapped short. Why the difference? It relates to the fact that the ID/key property has many important roles to play in the O/R mapping process (which is why it gets a special XML tag in the mapping document, rather than being just another property). Although we left it out in our specification, one of the choices you need to make when setting up an ID is to pick a special value to indicate that a particular instance has not yet been saved into the database. Leaving out this unsaved-value attribute, as we did, tells Hibernate to use its default interpretation, which is that unsaved values are indicated by an ID of null. Since native int values can't be null, they must be wrapped in a java.lang.Integer, and Hibernate took care of this for us.

When it comes to the volume property, Hibernate has no special need or use for it, so it trusts us to know what we're doing. If we want to be able to store null values for volume, perhaps to indicate "no change," we need to explicitly use java.lang.Short rather than short in our mapping document. (Had we not been sneakily pointing out this difference, our example would be better off explicitly using java.lang.Integer in our ID mapping too, just for clarity.)

Another thing you might notice about these field declarations is that their JavaDoc is quite generic—you may be wondering what happened to the "field-description" meta tags we put in the mapping document for playTime, added and volume. It turns out they appear only later, in the JavaDoc for the getter methods. They are not used in the setters, the actual field declarations, nor as @param entries for the constructor. As an avid user of a code-completing Java editor, I count on pop-up JavaDoc as I fill in arguments to method calls, so I'm a little disappointed by this limitation. Of course, since this is an open source project, any of us can get involved and propose or undertake this simple fix. Indeed, you may find this already remedied by the time you read this book. Once robust field and parameter documentation is in place, I'd definitely advocate always providing a brief but accurate field-description entry for your properties.

I know, I'm a perfectionist. I only bother to pick nits because I think Hibernate is so useful!

After the field declarations come a trio of constructors. The first (line 35) establishes values for all properties, the second (line 44) allows instantiation without any arguments (this is required if you want the class to be usable as a bean, such as on a Java Server Page, a very common use for data classes like this), and the last (line 48) fills in just the values we've indicated must not be null. Notice that none of the constructors set the value of id; this is the responsibility of Hibernate when we get the object out of the database, or insert it for the first time.

Consistent with that, the setId() method on line 57 is protected, as requested in our id mapping. The rest of the getters and setters are not surprising; this is all pretty much boilerplate code (which we've all written too many times), which is why it's so nice to be able to have the Hibernate extensions generate it for us.

WARNING

If you want to use Hibernate's generated code as a starting point and then add some business logic or other features to the generated class, be aware that all your changes will be silently discarded the next time you run the code generator. In such a project you will want to be sure the hand-tweaked classes are not regenerated by any Ant build target.

Even though we're having Hibernate generate our data classes in this example, it's important to point out that the getters and setters it creates are more than a nice touch. You *need* to put these in your persistent classes for any properties you want to persist, since Hibernate's fundamental persistence architecture is based on reflective access to Java-Beans™-style properties. They don't need to be public if you don't want them to; Hibernate has ways of getting at even properties declared protected or private, but they do need accessor methods. Think of it as enforcing good object design; the Hibernate team wants to keep the implementation details of actual instance variables cleanly separated from the persistence mechanism.

Cooking Up a Schema

That was pretty easy, wasn't it? You'll be happy to learn that creating database tables is a very similar process. As with code generation, you've already done most of the work in coming up with the mapping document. All that's left is to set up and run the schema generation tool.

How do I do that?

The first step is something we alluded to in Chapter 1. We need to tell Hibernate the database we're going to be using, so it knows the specific "dialect" of SQL to use. SQL is a standard, yes, but every database goes beyond it in certain directions and has a specific set of features and limitations that affect real-life applications. To cope with this reality, Hibernate provides a set of classes that encapsulate the unique features of common database environments, in the package `net.sf.hibernate.dialect`. You just need to tell it which one you want to use. (And if you want to work with a database that isn't yet supported "out of the box," you can implement your own dialect.)

In our case, we're working with HSQLDB, so we want to use `HSQLDialect`. The easiest way to configure Hibernate is to create a properties file named *hibernate.properties* and put it at the root level somewhere in the class path. Create this file at the top level of your *src* directory, and put the lines shown in Example 2-4 into it.

Example 2-4. Setting up *hibernate.properties*

```
hibernate.dialect=net.sf.hibernate.dialect.HSQLDialect
hibernate.connection.driver_class=org.hsqldb.jdbcDriver
hibernate.connection.url=jdbc:hsqldb:data/music
hibernate.connection.username=sa
hibernate.connection.password=
```

You can use an XML format for the configuration information as well, but for the simple needs we have here, it doesn't buy you anything.

In addition to establishing the SQL dialect we are using, this tells Hibernate how to establish a connection to the database using the JDBC driver that ships as part of the HSQLDB database JAR archive, and that the data should live in the *data* directory we've created—in the database named *music*. The username and empty password (indeed, all these values) should be familiar from the experiment we ran at the end of Chapter 1.

TIP

Notice that we're using a relative path to specify the database filename. This works fine in our examples—we're using ant to control the working directory. If you copy this for use in a web application or other environment, though, you'll likely need to be more explicit about the location of the file.

You can put the properties file in other places, and give it other names, or use entirely different ways of getting the properties into Hibernate, but this is the default place it will look, so it's the path of least resistance (or, I guess, least runtime configuration).

We also need to add some new pieces to our build file, shown in Example 2-5. This is a somewhat substantial addition, because we need to compile our Java source in order to use the schema generation tool, which relies on reflection to get its details right. Add these targets right before the closing `</project>` tag at the end of *build.xml*.

Example 2-5. Ant build file additions for compilation and schema generation

```
1    <!-- Create our runtime subdirectories and copy resources into them -->
2    <target name="prepare" description="Sets up build structures">
3      <mkdir dir="${class.root}"/>
4
5      <!-- Copy our property files and O/R mappings for use at runtime -->
6      <copy todir="${class.root}" >
7        <fileset dir="${source.root}" >
8          <include name="**/*.properties"/>
9          <include name="**/*.hbm.xml"/>
10       </fileset>
11     </copy>
12   </target>
13
14   <!-- Compile the java source of the project -->
15   <target name="compile" depends="prepare"
16         description="Compiles all Java classes">
17     <javac srcdir="${source.root}"
18           destdir="${class.root}"
19           debug="on"
20           optimize="off"
21           deprecation="on">
22       <classpath refid="project.class.path"/>
23     </javac>
24   </target>
25
26   <!-- Generate the schemas for all mapping files in our class tree -->
27   <target name="schema" depends="compile"
28         description="Generate DB schema from the O/R mapping files">
29
30     <!-- Teach Ant how to use Hibernate's schema generation tool -->
31     <taskdef name="schemaexport"
32             classname="net.sf.hibernate.tool.hbm2ddl.SchemaExportTask"
33             classpathref="project.class.path"/>
34
35     <schemaexport properties="${class.root}/hibernate.properties"
36                 quiet="no" text="no" drop="no" delimiter=";">
37       <fileset dir="${class.root}">
38         <include name="**/*.hbm.xml"/>
39       </fileset>
40     </schemaexport>
41   </target>
```

First we add a `prepare` target that is intended to be used by other targets more than from the command line. Its purpose is to create, if necessary, the *classes* directory into which we're going to compile, and then copy any properties and mapping files found in the *src* directory hierarchy to corresponding directories in the *classes* hierarchy. This hierarchical copy operation (using the special "**/*" pattern) is a nice feature of Ant, enabling us to define and edit resources alongside to the source files that use them, while making those resources available at runtime via the class loader.

The aptly named compile target at line 14 uses the built-in java task to compile all the Java source files found in the *src* tree to the *classes* tree. Happily, this task also supports the project class path we've set up, so the compiler can find all the libraries we're using. The depends="prepare" attribute in the target definition tells Ant that before running the compile target, prepare must be run. Ant manages dependencies so that when you're building multiple targets with related dependencies, they are executed in the right order, and each dependency gets executed only once, even if it is mentioned by multiple targets.

If you're accustomed to using shell scripts to compile a lot of Java source, you'll be surprised by how quickly the compilation happens. Ant invokes the Java compiler within the same virtual machine that it is using, so there is no process startup delay for each compilation.

Finally, after all this groundwork, we can write the target we really wanted to! The schema target (line 26) depends on compile, so all our Java classes will be compiled and available for inspection when the schema generator runs. It uses taskdef internally at line 31 to define the schemaexport task that runs the Hibernate schema export tool, in the same way we provided access to the code generation tool at the top of the file. It then invokes this tool and tells it to generate the database schema associated with any mapping documents found in the *classes* tree.

There are a number of parameters you can give the schema export tool to configure the way it works. In this example (at line 35) we're telling it to display the SQL it runs so we can watch what it's doing (quiet="no"), to actually interact with the database and create the schema rather than simply writing out a DDL file we could import later or simply deleting the schema (text="no", drop="no"). For more details about these and other configuration options, consult the Hibernate reference manual.

TIP

You may be wondering why the taskdef for the schema update tool is inside our schema target, rather than at the top of the build file, next to the one for hbm2java. Well, I wanted it up there too, but I ran into a snag that's worth explaining. I got strange error messages the first time I tried to build the schema target, complaining there was no *hibernate.properties* on the class path and our compiled Track class couldn't be found. When I ran it again, it worked. Some detective work using **ant -verbose** revealed that if the *classes* directory didn't exist when the taskdef was encountered, Ant helpfully removed it from the class path. Since a taskdef can't have its own dependencies, the solution is to move it into the schema target, giving it the benefit of that target's dependencies, ensuring the *classes* directory exists by the time the taskdef is processed.

With these additions, we're ready to generate the schema for our TRACK table.

WARNING

You might think the drop="no" setting in our schema task means you can use it to update the schema—it won't drop the tables, right? Alas, this is a misleading parameter name: it means it won't *just* drop the tables, rather it will go ahead and generate the schema *after* dropping them. Much as you want to avoid the codegen task after making any changes to the generated Java source, you mustn't export the schema if you've put any data into the database. Luckily, there is another tool you can use for incremental schema updates that works much the same way, as long as your JDBC driver is powerful enough. This SchemaUpdate tool can be used with an Ant taskdef too.

Because we've asked the schema export task not to be "quiet," we want it to generate some log entries for us. In order for that to work, we need to configure log4j, the logging environment used by Hibernate. The easiest way to do this is to make a *log4j.properties* file available at the root of the class path. We can take advantage of our existing prepare target to copy this from the *src* to the *classes* directory at the same time it copies Hibernate's properties. Create a file named *log4j.properties* in the *src* directory with the content shown in Example 2-6. An easy way to do this is to copy the file out of the *src* directory in the Hibernate distribution you downloaded, since it's provided for use by their own examples. If you're typing it in yourself, you can skip the blocks that are commented out; they are provided to suggest useful logging alternatives.

Example 2-6. The logging configuration file, *log4j.properties*

```
### direct log messages to stdout ###
log4j.appender.stdout=org.apache.log4j.ConsoleAppender
log4j.appender.stdout.Target=System.out
log4j.appender.stdout.layout=org.apache.log4j.PatternLayout
log4j.appender.stdout.layout.ConversionPattern=%d{ABSOLUTE} %5p %c{1}:%L - %m%n

### direct messages to file hibernate.log ###
#log4j.appender.file=org.apache.log4j.FileAppender
#log4j.appender.file.File=hibernate.log
#log4j.appender.file.layout=org.apache.log4j.PatternLayout
#log4j.appender.file.layout.ConversionPattern=%d{ABSOLUTE} %5p %c{1}:%L - %m%n

### set log levels - for more verbose logging change 'info' to 'debug' ###

log4j.rootLogger=warn, stdout
```

Example 2-6. *The logging configuration file, log4j.properties (continued)*

```
log4j.logger.net.sf.hibernate=info

### log just the SQL
#log4j.logger.net.sf.hibernate.SQL=debug

### log JDBC bind parameters ###
log4j.logger.net.sf.hibernate.type=info

### log schema export/update ###
log4j.logger.net.sf.hibernate.tool.hbm2ddl=debug

### log cache activity ###
#log4j.logger.net.sf.hibernate.cache=debug

### enable the following line if you want to track down connection ###
### leakages when using DriverManagerConnectionProvider ###
#log4j.logger.net.sf.hibernate.connection.DriverManagerConnectionProvider=trace
```

TIP

With the log configuration in place, you might want to edit the codegen target in *build.xml* so that it, too, depends on our new prepare target. This will ensure logging is configured whenever we use it, preventing the warnings we saw when first running it. As noted in the tip about class paths and task definitions in the previous section, though, to make it work the very first time you'll have to move the taskdef for hbm2java inside the codegen target, in the same way we put schemaexport inside the schema target.

Time to make a schema! From the project directory, execute the command **ant schema**. You'll see output similar to Example 2-7 as the *classes* directory is created and populated with resources, the Java source is compiled,[*] and the schema generator is run.

Example 2-7. *Output from building the schema using HSQLDB's embedded database server*

```
% ant schema
Buildfile: build.xml

prepare:
    [mkdir] Created dir: /Users/jim/Documents/Work/OReilly/Hibernate/Examples/
ch02/classes
```

---

[*] We're assuming you've already generated the code shown in Example 2-3, or there won't be any Java source to compile, and the schema generation will fail. The schema target doesn't invoke codegen to automatically generate code, in case you've manually extended any of your generated classes.

Example 2-7. Output from building the schema using HSQLDB's embedded database server (continued)

```
     [copy] Copying 3 files to /Users/jim/Documents/Work/OReilly/Hibernate/
Examples/ch02/classes

compile:
     [javac] Compiling 1 source file to /Users/jim/Documents/Work/OReilly/
Hibernate/Examples/ch02/classes

schema:
[schemaexport] 23:50:36,165  INFO Environment:432 - Hibernate 2.1.1
[schemaexport] 23:50:36,202  INFO Environment:466 - loaded properties from
resource hibernate.properties: {hibernate.connection.username=sa, hibernate.
connection.password=, hibernate.cglib.use_reflection_optimizer=true, hibernate.
dialect=net.sf.hibernate.dialect.HSQLDialect, hibernate.connection.url=jdbc:
hsqldb:data/music, hibernate.connection.driver_class=org.hsqldb.jdbcDriver}
[schemaexport] 23:50:36,310  INFO Environment:481 - using CGLIB reflection
optimizer
[schemaexport] 23:50:36,384  INFO Configuration:166 - Mapping file: /Users/jim/
Documents/Work/OReilly/Hibernate/Examples/ch02/classes/com/oreilly/hh/Track.hbm.
xml
[schemaexport] 23:50:37,409  INFO Binder:225 - Mapping class: com.oreilly.hh.
Track -> TRACK
[schemaexport] 23:50:37,928  INFO Dialect:82 - Using dialect: net.sf.hibernate.
dialect.HSQLDialect
[schemaexport] 23:50:37,942  INFO Configuration:584 - processing one-to-many
association mappings
[schemaexport] 23:50:37,947  INFO Configuration:593 - processing one-to-one
association property references
[schemaexport] 23:50:37,956  INFO Configuration:618 - processing foreign key
constraints
[schemaexport] 23:50:38,113  INFO Configuration:584 - processing one-to-many
association mappings
[schemaexport] 23:50:38,124  INFO Configuration:593 - processing one-to-one
association property references
[schemaexport] 23:50:38,132  INFO Configuration:618 - processing foreign key
constraints
[schemaexport] 23:50:38,149  INFO SchemaExport:98 - Running hbm2ddl schema export
[schemaexport] 23:50:38,154  INFO SchemaExport:117 - exporting generated schema
to database
[schemaexport] 23:50:38,232  INFO DriverManagerConnectionProvider:41 - Using
Hibernate built-in connection pool (not for production use!)
[schemaexport] 23:50:38,238  INFO DriverManagerConnectionProvider:42 - Hibernate
connection pool size: 20
[schemaexport] 23:50:38,278  INFO DriverManagerConnectionProvider:71 - using
driver: org.hsqldb.jdbcDriver at URL: jdbc:hsqldb:data/music
[schemaexport] 23:50:38,283  INFO DriverManagerConnectionProvider:72 - connection
properties: {user=sa, password=}
[schemaexport] drop table TRACK if exists
[schemaexport] 23:50:39,083 DEBUG SchemaExport:132 - drop table TRACK if exists
[schemaexport] create table TRACK (
[schemaexport]    TRACK_ID INTEGER NOT NULL IDENTITY,
[schemaexport]    title VARCHAR(255) not null,
[schemaexport]    filePath VARCHAR(255) not null,
[schemaexport]    playTime TIME,
```

Example 2-7. Output from building the schema using HSQLDB's embedded database server (continued)

```
[schemaexport]    added DATE,
[schemaexport]    volume SMALLINT
[schemaexport] )
[schemaexport] 23:50:39,113 DEBUG SchemaExport:149 - create table TRACK (
[schemaexport]    TRACK_ID INTEGER NOT NULL IDENTITY,
[schemaexport]    title VARCHAR(255) not null,
[schemaexport]    filePath VARCHAR(255) not null,
[schemaexport]    playTime TIME,
[schemaexport]    added DATE,
[schemaexport]    volume SMALLINT
[schemaexport] )
[schemaexport] 23:50:39,142  INFO SchemaExport:160 - schema export complete
[schemaexport] 23:50:39,178  INFO DriverManagerConnectionProvider:137 - cleaning
up connection pool: jdbc:hsqldb:data/music

BUILD SUCCESSFUL
Total time: 10 seconds
```

Toward the end of the schemaexport section you can see the actual SQL used by Hibernate to create the TRACK table. If you look at the start of the *music.script* file in the *data* directory, you'll see it's been incorporated into the database. For a slightly more friendly (and perhaps convincing) way to see it, execute **ant db** to fire up the HSQLDB graphical interface, as shown in Figure 2-1.

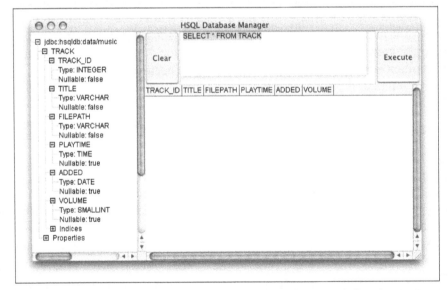

Figure 2-1. The database interface with our new TRACK table expanded, and a query

What just happened?

We were able to use Hibernate to create a data table in which we can persist instances of the Java class it created for us. We didn't have to type a single line of SQL or Java! Of course, our table is still empty at this point. Let's change that! The next chapter will look at the stuff you probably most want to see: using Hibernate from within a Java program to turn objects into database entries and vice versa.

It's about time? Yeah, I suppose. But at least you didn't have to figure out all these steps from scratch!

Before diving into that cool task, it's worth taking a moment to reflect on how much we've been able to accomplish with a couple of XML and properties files. Hopefully you're starting to see the power and convenience that make Hibernate so exciting.

What about...

...Other approaches to ID generation? Keys that are globally unique across a database or the world? Hibernate can support a variety of methods for picking the keys for objects it stores in the database. This is controlled using the generator tag, line 15 in Example 2-1. In this example we told Hibernate to use the most natural kind of keys for the type of database that it happens to be using. Other alternatives include the popular "hi/lo" algorithm, global UUIDs, leaving it entirely up to your Java code, and more. See the "generator" section in the Basic O/R Mapping chapter of the Hibernate reference documentation for details. And, as usual, if none of the built-in choices are perfect for your needs, you can supply your own class to do it exactly how you'd like, implementing the interface net.sf.hibernate.id.IdentifierGenerator and supplying your class name in the generator tag.

Connecting Hibernate to MySQL

If you were skimming through this chapter (or, more likely, the table of contents) you may not have even noticed that Hibernate connected to and manipulated a database in the previous section, "Cooking Up a Schema." Since working with databases is the whole point of Hibernate, it makes this as easy as possible. Once you've set up a configuration file like the one in Example 2-4, the schema generation tool can get in and work with your database, and your Java code can use it for persistence sessions as demonstrated in Chapter 3.

This example assumes you've already got a working MySQL instance installed and running, since explaining how to do that would be quite a detour.

In the interest of further clarifying this aspect of working with Hibernate, let's take a look at what we'd change in that example to set up a connection with the popular, free, and open source MySQL database (available from *http://www.mysql.com*).

How do I do that?

Connect to your MySQL server and set up a new database to play with, along the lines of Example 2-8.

Example 2-8. Setting up the MySQL database *notebook_db* as a Hibernate playground

```
% mysql -u root -p
Enter password:
Welcome to the MySQL monitor.  Commands end with ; or \g.
Your MySQL connection id is 764 to server version: 3.23.44-Max-log

Type 'help;' or '\h' for help. Type '\c' to clear the buffer.

mysql> CREATE DATABASE notebook_db;
Query OK, 1 row affected (0.00 sec)

mysql> GRANT ALL ON notebook_db.* TO jim IDENTIFIED BY "s3cret";
Query OK, 0 rows affected (0.20 sec)

mysql> quit;
Bye
```

Hopefully you'll use a less guessable password than this in your real databases!

Make a note of the database name you create, as well as the username and password that can access to it. These will need to be entered into *hibernate.properties*, as shown in Example 2-9.

Next, you'll need a JDBC driver capable of connecting to MySQL. If you're already using MySQL for your Java projects, you'll have one. Otherwise, you can download Connector/J from *http://www.mysql.com/downloads/api-jdbc-stable.html*. However you obtain it, copy the driver library jar (which will be named something like *mysql-connector-java-3.0.10-stable-bin.jar*) to your project's *lib* directory alongside the HSQLDB, Hibernate, and other libraries that are already there. It's fine to have drivers for several different databases available to your code; they won't conflict with each other, since the configuration file specifies which driver class to use.

Speaking of which, it's time to edit *hibernate.properties* to use the new driver and database we've just made available. Example 2-9 shows how it is set up to connect to my MySQL instance using the database created in Example 2-8. You'll need to tweak these values to correspond to your own server, database, and the login credentials you chose. (If you're using MM.MySQL, the older incarnation of the MySQL JDBC driver, the driver_class will need to be com.mysql.jdbc.Driver.)

Example 2-9. Changes to *hibernate.properties* to connect to the new MySQL database

```
hibernate.dialect=net.sf.hibernate.dialect.MySQLDialect
hibernate.connection.driver_class=com.mysql.jdbc.Driver
hibernate.connection.url=jdbc:mysql://slant.reseune.pvt/notebook_db
hibernate.connection.username=jim
hibernate.connection.password=s3cret
```

The URL on the third line will need to reflect your server; you won't be able to resolve my private internal domain name, let alone route to it.

Once this is all set, you can rerun the schema creation example that was set up in the previous section. This time it will build the schema on your MySQL server rather than in the embedded HSQLDB world. You'll see output like that in Example 2-10.

Example 2-10. Schema creation when connecting to MySQL

```
% ant schema
Buildfile: build.xml

prepare:

compile:

schema:
[schemaexport] 23:02:13,614  INFO Environment:462 - Hibernate 2.1.2
[schemaexport] 23:02:13,659  INFO Environment:496 - loaded properties from
resource hibernate.properties: {hibernate.connection.username=jim, hibernate.
connection.password=s3cret, hibernate.cglib.use_reflection_optimizer=true,
hibernate.dialect=net.sf.hibernate.dialect.MySQLDialect, hibernate.connection.
url=jdbc:mysql://slant.reseune.pvt/notebook_db, hibernate.connection.driver_
class=com.mysql.jdbc.Driver}
[schemaexport] 23:02:13,711  INFO Environment:519 - using CGLIB reflection
optimizer
[schemaexport] 23:02:13,819  INFO Configuration:166 - Mapping file: /Users/jim/
Documents/Work/OReilly/Hibernate/Examples/ch02/classes/com/oreilly/hh/Track.hbm.xml
[schemaexport] 23:02:15,568  INFO Binder:229 - Mapping class: com.oreilly.hh.
Track -> TRACK
[schemaexport] 23:02:16,164  INFO Dialect:82 - Using dialect: net.sf.hibernate.
dialect.MySQLDialect
[schemaexport] 23:02:16,175  INFO Configuration:595 - processing one-to-many
association mappings
[schemaexport] 23:02:16,188  INFO Configuration:604 - processing one-to-one
association property references
[schemaexport] 23:02:16,209  INFO Configuration:629 - processing foreign key
constraints
[schemaexport] 23:02:16,429  INFO Configuration:595 - processing one-to-many
association mappings
[schemaexport] 23:02:16,436  INFO Configuration:604 - processing one-to-one
association property references
```

Example 2-10. *Schema creation when connecting to MySQL (continued)*

```
[schemaexport] 23:02:16,440  INFO Configuration:629 - processing foreign key
constraints
[schemaexport] 23:02:16,470  INFO SchemaExport:98 - Running hbm2ddl schema export
[schemaexport] 23:02:16,488  INFO SchemaExport:117 - exporting generated schema
to database
[schemaexport] 23:02:16,543  INFO DriverManagerConnectionProvider:41 - Using
Hibernate built-in connection pool (not for production use!)
[schemaexport] 23:02:16,549  INFO DriverManagerConnectionProvider:42 - Hibernate
connection pool size: 20
[schemaexport] 23:02:16,583  INFO DriverManagerConnectionProvider:71 - using
driver: com.mysql.jdbc.Driver at URL: jdbc:mysql://slant.reseune.pvt/notebook_db
[schemaexport] 23:02:16,597  INFO DriverManagerConnectionProvider:72 - connection
properties: {user=jim, password=s3cret}
[schemaexport] drop table if exists TRACK
[schemaexport] 23:02:18,129 DEBUG SchemaExport:132 - drop table if exists TRACK
[schemaexport] create table TRACK (
[schemaexport]     TRACK_ID INTEGER NOT NULL AUTO_INCREMENT,
[schemaexport]     title VARCHAR(255) not null,
[schemaexport]     filePath VARCHAR(255) not null,
[schemaexport]     playTime TIME,
[schemaexport]     added DATE,
[schemaexport]     volume SMALLINT,
[schemaexport]     primary key (Track_id)
[schemaexport] )
[schemaexport] 23:02:18,181 DEBUG SchemaExport:149 - create table TRACK (
[schemaexport]     TRACK_ID INTEGER NOT NULL AUTO_INCREMENT,
[schemaexport]     title VARCHAR(255) not null,
[schemaexport]     filePath VARCHAR(255) not null,
[schemaexport]     playTime TIME,
[schemaexport]     added DATE,
[schemaexport]     volume SMALLINT,
[schemaexport]     primary key (Track_id)
[schemaexport] )
[schemaexport] 23:02:18,311  INFO SchemaExport:160 - schema export complete
[schemaexport] 23:02:18,374  INFO DriverManagerConnectionProvider:137 - cleaning
up connection pool: jdbc:mysql://slant.reseune.pvt/notebook_db

BUILD SUCCESSFUL
Total time: 9 seconds
```

What just happened?

Hibernate configured itself to work with MySQL's specific features, examined the mapping document for our Track class, connected to the MySQL server, and executed the commands necessary to build a database schema for persisting Track instances.

It's interesting to compare Example 2-11 with Example 2-7. Most of the output is the same, but there are subtle differences in the SQL used to actually create the table. This is what Hibernate means by SQL "dialects."

Back on the server, you can fire up the MySQL client again, and confirm that the Track mapping schema has been created.

Example 2-11. Checking the newly created MySQL schema

```
% mysql -u jim -p
Enter password:
Welcome to the MySQL monitor.  Commands end with ; or \g.
Your MySQL connection id is 772 to server version: 3.23.44-Max-log

Type 'help;' or '\h' for help. Type '\c' to clear the buffer.

mysql> USE notebook_db
Database changed
mysql> SHOW TABLES;
+----------------------+
| Tables_in_notebook_db |
+----------------------+
| TRACK                |
+----------------------+
1 row in set (0.03 sec)

mysql> DESCRIBE TRACK;
+----------+--------------+------+-----+---------+----------------+
| Field    | Type         | Null | Key | Default | Extra          |
+----------+--------------+------+-----+---------+----------------+
| TRACK_ID | int(11)      |      | PRI | NULL    | auto_increment |
| title    | varchar(255) |      |     |         |                |
| filePath | varchar(255) |      |     |         |                |
| playTime | time         | YES  |     | NULL    |                |
| added    | date         | YES  |     | NULL    |                |
| volume   | smallint(6)  | YES  |     | NULL    |                |
+----------+--------------+------+-----+---------+----------------+
6 rows in set (0.02 sec)

mysql> SELECT * FROM TRACK;
Empty set (0.00 sec)

mysql> quit;
Bye
```

It's not surprising to find the table empty. We'll investigate how to populate it with data in the first part of Chapter 3.

If you've followed this example and set up a MySQL database, and you'd prefer to continue working with it throughout the rest of the book, feel free to do so, but bear in mind you'll need to know how to look at the results of the examples yourself. The text will assume you're still working with HSQLDB, and it will show you how to check your progress in that context. You will also see slight differences in the schema, as databases all have slightly different column types and features. Apart from these minor details, it really makes no difference what database you're using—that's part of the appeal of an O/R mapping layer like Hibernate.

If you do want to switch back to HSQLDB for the ease of following the discussion, change your *hibernate.properties* back to the values shown in Example 2-4.

What about...

...Connecting to Oracle, or another favorite, shared, or legacy database that doesn't happen to be MySQL or HSQLDB? You've probably figured out that it's just as easy. All you need to do is change the `hibernate.dialect` setting in your *hibernate.properties* to reflect the kind of database you want to use. There are many dialects available, covering every free and commercial database I can think of. These built-in dialects are listed in Appendix C. If you need to work with a more obscure database, you may have to write your own dialect to support it, but that seems unlikely (and check to see if anyone's already started that effort).

Once you've chosen the dialect, you'll also need to set the `hibernate.connection` properties (driver, URL, username, and password—the other entries in Example 2-4 and Example 2-9) to the proper values for establishing a JDBC connection to your chosen database environment. If you're porting an existing project to use Hibernate, you'll be able to obtain these from the code or configuration of that project. And, naturally, you'll need to put the database's JDBC driver into your project's library directory.

Of course, if you're connecting to an existing or shared database, you won't be using Hibernate to create the schema. Instead, you'll write the mapping document to reflect the existing schema, either by hand or with the help of a tool like Middlegen (*http://boss.bekk.no/boss/middlegen*), and then start working with the data in the form of persistent objects, as described in Chapter 3.

You can even use Hibernate to talk to multiple databases at the same time; you just need to create multiple `SessionFactory` instances with separate configurations. This goes beyond the simple, automatic configuration we demonstrate in Chapter 3, but there are examples in the Hibernate reference documentation. Of course, a persistent object can only be associated with a single session at a time, which means it can only be linked to a single database at once. With clever, careful coding, though, you can copy or move objects between different database systems, even with a different schema to represent them. That's *way* out of scope for this notebook, though!

Harnessing Hibernate

All right, we've set up a whole bunch of infrastructure, defined an object/relational mapping, and used it to create a matching Java class and database table. But what does that buy us? It's time to see how easy it is to work with persistent data from your Java code.

Creating Persistent Objects

Let's start by creating some objects in Java and persisting them to the database, so we can see how they turn into rows and columns for us. Because of the way we've organized our mapping document and properties file, it's extremely easy to configure the Hibernate session factory and get things rolling.

To get started, set up the Hibernate environment and use it to turn some new Track instances into corresponding rows in the database table.

How do I do that?

This discussion assumes you've created the schema and generated Java code by following the examples in Chapter 2. If you haven't, you can start by downloading the examples archive from this book's web site, jumping in to the *ch03* directory, and copying in the third-party libraries as instructed in Chapter 1. Once you've done that, use the commands **ant codegen** followed by **ant schema** to set up the generated Java code and database schema on which this example is based. As with the other examples, these commands should be issued in a shell/command window whose current working directory is the top of your project tree, containing Ant's *build.xml* file.

We'll start with a simple example class, CreateTest, containing the necessary imports and housekeeping code to bring up the Hibernate environment and create some Track instances that can be persisted using the XML mapping document we started with. The source is shown in Example 3-1.

The examples in most chapters build on the previous ones, so if you are skipping around, you'll really want to download the sample code.

Example 3-1. *CreateTest.java*

```
1   package com.oreilly.hh;
2
3   import net.sf.hibernate.*;
4   import net.sf.hibernate.cfg.Configuration;
5
6   import java.sql.Time;
7   import java.util.Date;
8
9   /**
10   * Create sample data, letting Hibernate persist it for us.
11   */
12  public class CreateTest {
13
14      public static void main(String args[]) throws Exception {
15          // Create a configuration based on the properties file we've put
16          // in the standard place.
17          Configuration config = new Configuration();
18
19          // Tell it about the classes we want mapped, taking advantage of
20          // the way we've named their mapping documents.
21          config.addClass(Track.class);
22
23          // Get the session factory we can use for persistence
24          SessionFactory sessionFactory = config.buildSessionFactory();
25
26          // Ask for a session using the JDBC information we've configured
27          Session session = sessionFactory.openSession();
28          Transaction tx = null;
29          try {
30              // Create some data and persist it
31              tx = session.beginTransaction();
32
33              Track track = new Track("Russian Trance",
34                                      "vol2/album610/track02.mp3",
35                                      Time.valueOf("00:03:30"), new Date(),
36                                      (short)0);
37              session.save(track);
38
39              track = new Track("Video Killed the Radio Star",
40                                "vol2/album611/track12.mp3",
41                                Time.valueOf("00:03:49"), new Date(),
42                                (short)0);
43              session.save(track);
44
45
```

Example 3-1. *CreateTest.java* (continued)

```
46              track = new Track("Gravity's Angel",
47                          "vol2/album175/track03.mp3",
48                          Time.valueOf("00:06:06"), new Date(),
49                          (short)0);
50          session.save(track);
51
52          // We're done; make our changes permanent
53          tx.commit();
54
55      } catch (Exception e) {
56          if (tx != null) {
57              // Something went wrong; discard all partial changes
58              tx.rollback();
59          }
60          throw e;
61      } finally {
62          // No matter what, close the session
63          session.close();
64      }
65
66      // Clean up after ourselves
67      sessionFactory.close();
68      }
69  }
```

With all we've got in place by now it's quite easy to tell Ant how to run this test. Add the target shown in Example 3-2 right before the closing </project> tag at the end of *build.xml*.

Example 3-2. Ant target to invoke our data creation test

```
<target name="ctest" description="Creates and persists some sample data"
        depends="compile">
  <java classname="com.oreilly.hh.CreateTest" fork="true">
    <classpath refid="project.class.path"/>
  </java>
</target>
```

All right, we're ready to create some data! Example 3-3 shows the results of invoking the new ctest target. Its dependency on the compile target ensures the CreateTest class gets compiled before we try to use it. The output for ctest itself shows the logging emitted by Hibernate as the environment and mappings are set up and the connection is shut back down.

Example 3-3. Invoking the CreateTest class

```
% ant ctest
Buildfile: build.xml

prepare:
```

Example 3-3. Invoking the CreateTest class (continued)

```
compile:
    [javac] Compiling 1 source file to /Users/jim/Documents/Work/OReilly/
Hibernate/Examples/ch03/classes

ctest:
    [java] 00:07:46,376  INFO Environment:432 - Hibernate 2.1.1
    [java] 00:07:46,514  INFO Environment:466 - loaded properties from resource
hibernate.properties: {hibernate.connection.username=sa, hibernate.connection.
password=, hibernate.cglib.use_reflection_optimizer=true, hibernate.dialect=net.
sf.hibernate.dialect.HSQLDialect, hibernate.connection.url=jdbc:hsqldb:data/
music, hibernate.connection.driver_class=org.hsqldb.jdbcDriver}
    [java] 00:07:46,644  INFO Environment:481 - using CGLIB reflection optimizer
    [java] 00:07:46,691  INFO Configuration:318 - Mapping resource: com/oreilly/
hh/Track.hbm.xml
    [java] 00:07:50,686  INFO Binder:225 - Mapping class: com.oreilly.hh.Track
-> TRACK
    [java] 00:07:51,620  INFO Configuration:584 - processing one-to-many
association mappings
    [java] 00:07:51,627  INFO Configuration:593 - processing one-to-one
association property references
    [java] 00:07:51,628  INFO Configuration:618 - processing foreign key
constraints
    [java] 00:07:51,869  INFO Dialect:82 - Using dialect: net.sf.hibernate.
dialect.HSQLDialect
    [java] 00:07:51,886  INFO SettingsFactory:62 - Use outer join fetching: false
    [java] 00:07:51,966  INFO DriverManagerConnectionProvider:41 - Using
Hibernate built-in connection pool (not for production use!)
    [java] 00:07:52,036  INFO DriverManagerConnectionProvider:42 - Hibernate
connection pool size: 20
    [java] 00:07:52,117  INFO DriverManagerConnectionProvider:71 - using driver:
org.hsqldb.jdbcDriver at URL: jdbc:hsqldb:data/music
    [java] 00:07:52,135  INFO DriverManagerConnectionProvider:72 - connection
properties: {user=sa, password=}
    [java] 00:07:52,171  INFO TransactionManagerLookupFactory:33 - No
TransactionManagerLookup configured (in JTA environment, use of process level
read-write cache is not recommended)
    [java] 00:07:53,497  INFO SettingsFactory:89 - Use scrollable result sets:
true
    [java] 00:07:53,504  INFO SettingsFactory:99 - Query language substitutions: {}
    [java] 00:07:53,507  INFO SettingsFactory:110 - cache provider:
net.sf.ehcache.hibernate.Provider
    [java] 00:07:53,528  INFO Configuration:1057 - instantiating and configuring
caches
    [java] 00:07:54,533  INFO SessionFactoryImpl:119 - building session factory
    [java] 00:07:56,721  INFO SessionFactoryObjectFactory:82 - no JNDI name
configured
    [java] 00:07:57,357  INFO SessionFactoryImpl:527 - closing
    [java] 00:07:57,370  INFO DriverManagerConnectionProvider:137 - cleaning up
connection pool: jdbc:hsqldb:data/music

BUILD SUCCESSFUL
Total time: 23 seconds
```

What just happened?

Our test class fired up Hibernate, loaded the mapping information for the `Track` class, opened a persistence session to the associated HSQLDB database, and used that to create some instances and persist them in the `TRACK` table. Then it shut down the session and closed the database connection, ensuring the data was saved.

After running this test, you can use **ant db** to take a look at the contents of the database. You should find three rows in the `TRACK` table now, as shown in Figure 3-1. (Type your query in the text box at the top of the window and click the Execute button. You can get a command skeleton and syntax documentation by choosing Command → Select in the menu bar.)

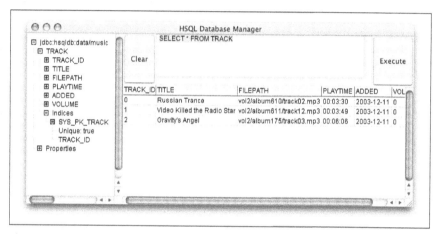

Figure 3-1. Test data persisted into the TRACK table

The first part of Example 3-1's code needs little explanation. Lines 3 and 4 import some useful Hibernate classes, including `Configuration`, which is used to set up the Hibernate environment. The `Time` and `Date` classes are used in our data objects to represent track playing times and creation timestamps. The only method we implement in `CreateTest` is the `main()` method that supports invocation from the command line.

When run, we start by creating a Hibernate `Configuration` object on line 17. Since we don't tell it otherwise, it looks for a file named *hibernate.properties* at the root level in the class path. It finds the one we created in the previous chapter (see Example 2-4), which tells it we're using HSQLDB, and how to find the database. Next line 21 requests mapping services for the `Track` class. Because we've placed the mapping file

Track.hbm.xml in the same package, and followed the standard naming convention, Hibernate is able to find and load it without requiring an explicit path. This approach is particularly handy when you want to distribute your application as a Jar archive, or when you are operating in a web application environment.

That's all the configuration we need in order to create and persist track data, so we're ready to create the SessionFactory on line 24. Its purpose is to provide us with Session objects, the main avenue for interaction with Hibernate. The SessionFactory is thread safe, and you only need one for your entire application. (To be more precise, you need one for each database environment for which you want persistence services; most applications therefore need only one.) Creating the session factory is a pretty expensive and slow operation, so you'll definitely want to share it throughout your application. It's trivial in a one-class application like this one, but the reference documentation provides some good examples of ways to do it in more realistic scenarios.

When it comes time to actually perform persistence, we ask the SessionFactory to open a Session for us (line 27), which establishes a JDBC connection to the database, and provides us with a context in which we can create, obtain, manipulate, and delete persistent objects. As long as the session is open, a connection to the database is maintained, and changes to the persistent objects associated with the session are tracked so they can be applied to the database when the session is closed. Conceptually you can think of a session as a "large scale transaction" between the persistent objects and the database, which may encompass several database-level transactions. Like a database transaction, though, you should not think about keeping your Hibernate session open over long periods of application existence (such as while you're waiting for user input). A single session is used for a specific and bounded operation in the application, something like populating the user interface or making a change that has been committed by the user. The next operation will use a new session. Also note that Session objects are not thread safe, so they cannot be shared between threads. Each thread needs to obtain its own session from the factory.

We need to look more closely at the lifecycle of mapped objects in Hibernate, and how this relates to sessions, because the terminology is rather specific and the concepts are quite important. A mapped object such as an instance of our Track class moves back and forth between two states with respect to Hibernate: *transient* and *persistent*. An object that is transient is

It's worth getting a solid understanding of the purposes and lifecycles of these objects. This notebook gives you just enough information to get started; you'll want to spend some time with the reference documentation and understand the examples in depth.

not associated with any session. When you first create a `Track` instance using `new()`, it is transient; unless you tell Hibernate to persist it, the object will vanish when it is garbage collected or your application terminates.

Passing a transient mapped object to a `Session`'s `save()` method causes it to become persistent. It will survive garbage collection and termination of the Java VM, staying available until it is explicitly deleted. (There is a related distinction between *entities* and *values* discussed at the beginning of Appendix A. Mapped objects that have been persisted are called entities, even if they do not currently exist as an instance in any virtual machine.) If you've got a persistent object and you call `Session`'s `delete()` method on it, the object transitions back to a transient state. The object still exists as an instance in your application, but it is no longer going to stay around unless you change your mind and save it again; it's ceased being an entity.

On the other hand, and this point is worth extra emphasis, if you haven't deleted an object (so it's still persistent), when you change its properties there is no need to save it again for those changes to be reflected in the database. Hibernate automatically tracks changes to any persistent objects and flushes those changes to the database at appropriate times. When you close the session, any pending changes are flushed.

Hang in there, we'll be back to the example soon!

An important but subtle point concerns the status of persistent objects you worked with in a session that has been closed, such as after you run a query to find all entities matching some criteria (you'll see how to do this in the upcoming section, "Finding Persistent Objects"). As noted above, you don't want to keep this session around longer than necessary to perform the database operation, so you close it once your queries are finished. What's the deal with the mapped objects you've loaded at this point? Well, they were persistent while the session was around, but once they are no longer associated with an active session (in this case because the session has been closed) they are not persistent any longer. Now, this doesn't mean that they no longer exist in the database; indeed, if you run the query again (assuming nobody has changed the data in the meantime), you'll get back the same set of objects; they're still entities. It simply means that there is not currently an active correspondence being maintained between the state of the objects in your virtual machine and the database. It is perfectly reasonable to carry on working with the objects. If you later need to make changes to the objects and you want the changes to "stick," you will open a new session and use it to save the changed objects. Because each entity has a unique ID, Hibernate has no problem figuring out how to link the transient objects back to the appropriate persistent state in the new session.

TIP

Of course, as with any environment in which you're making changes to an offline copy of information backed by a database, you need to think about application-level data integrity constraints. You may need to devise some higher-level locking or versioning protocol to support them. Hibernate can offer help with this task too, but the design and detailed implementation is up to you. The reference manual does strongly recommend the use of a version field, and there are several approaches available.

Armed with these concepts and terms, the remainder of the example is easy enough to understand. Line 31 sets up a database transaction using our open session. Within that, we create a few Track instances containing sample data and save them in the session (lines 33–50), turning them from transient instances into persistent entities. Finally, line 53 commits our transaction, atomically (as a single, indivisible unit) making all the database changes permanent. The try/catch/finally block wrapped around all this shows an important and useful idiom for working with transactions. If anything goes wrong, lines 56–60 will roll back the transaction and then bubble out the exception, leaving the database the way we found it. The session is closed in the finally portion at line 63, ensuring that this takes place whether we exit through the "happy path" of a successful commit, or via an exception that caused rollback. Either way, it gets closed as it should.

At the end of our method we also close the session factory itself on line 67. This is something you'd do in the "graceful shutdown" section of your application. In a web application environment, it would be in the appropriate lifecycle event handler.* In this simple example, when the main() method returns, the application is ending.

---

* If you're not familiar with these, read about the ServletContextListener interface in the Servlet 2.3 specification.

At this point it's worth pausing a moment to reflect on the fact that we wrote no code to connect to the database or to issue SQL commands. Looking back to the preceding chapter, we didn't even have to create the table ourselves, nor the Track object that encapsulates our data. Yet the query in Figure 3-1 shows nicely readable data representing the Java objects created and persisted by our short, simple test program. Hopefully you'll agree that this reflects very well on the power and convenience of Hibernate as a persistence service. For being free and lightweight, Hibernate can certainly do a lot for you, quickly and easily.

An alternate way of seeing the results of our persistence test is to simply look at the database itself. Since we're using HSQLDB, the database is stored in a highly human-readable format: the file *music.script* contains a series of SQL statements that are used to reconstruct the in-memory database structures when the database is opened. The end of the file contains our persisted objects, as shown in Example 3-4.

Example 3-4. Looking at the raw database file

```
% tail data/music.script
CREATE ALIAS ATAN FOR "java.lang.Math.atan"
CREATE ALIAS UPPER FOR "org.hsqldb.Library.ucase"
CREATE ALIAS ASCII FOR "org.hsqldb.Library.ascii"
CREATE ALIAS RAND FOR "java.lang.Math.random"
CREATE ALIAS LENGTH FOR "org.hsqldb.Library.length"
CREATE ALIAS ROUND FOR "org.hsqldb.Library.round"
CREATE ALIAS REPLACE FOR "org.hsqldb.Library.replace"
INSERT INTO TRACK VALUES(0,'Russian Trance','vol2/album610/track02.mp3',
'00:03:30','2003-12-11',0)
INSERT INTO TRACK VALUES(1,'Video Killed the Radio Star','vol2/album611/
track12.mp3','00:03:49','2003-12-11',0)
INSERT INTO TRACK VALUES(2,'Gravity''s Angel','vol2/album175/track03.mp3',
'00:06:06','2003-12-11',0)
```

The final three statements show our TRACK table rows. The aliases that come before them are part of the normal HSQLDB environment you get when creating a new database.

Tempted to learn more about HSQLDB? I won't try to stop you!

What about...

...Objects with relationships to other objects? Collections of objects? You're right, these are cases where persistence gets more challenging (and, if done right, valuable). Hibernate can handle associations like this just fine. In fact, there isn't any special effort involved on our part. We'll discuss this in Chapter 4. For now, let's look at how to retrieve objects that were persisted in earlier sessions.

Finding Persistent Objects

It's time to throw the giant lever into reverse and look at how you load data from a database into Java objects.

Use Hibernate Query Language to get an object-oriented view of the contents of your mapped database tables. These might have started out as objects persisted in a previous session, or they might be data that came from completely outside your application code.

How do I do that?

Example 3-5 shows a program that runs a simple query using the test data we just created. The overall structure will look very familiar, because all the Hibernate setup is the same as the previous program.

Example 3-5. *QueryTest.java*

```java
1   package com.oreilly.hh;
2
3   import net.sf.hibernate.*;
4   import net.sf.hibernate.cfg.Configuration;
5
6   import java.sql.Time;
7   import java.util.*;
8
9   /**
10   * Retrieve data as objects
11   */
12  public class QueryTest {
13
14      /**
15       * Retrieve any tracks that fit in the specified amount of time.
16       *
17       * @param length the maximum playing time for tracks to be returned.
18       * @param session the Hibernate session that can retrieve data.
19       * @return a list of {@link Track}s meeting the length restriction.
20       * @throws HibernateException if there is a problem.
21       */
22      public static List tracksNoLongerThan(Time length, Session session)
23          throws HibernateException
24      {
25          return session.find("from com.oreilly.hh.Track as track " +
26                              "where track.playTime <= ?",
27                              length, Hibernate.TIME);
28      }
29
30      /**
31       * Look up and print some tracks when invoked from the command line.
32       */
33      public static void main(String args[]) throws Exception {
34          // Create a configuration based on the properties file we've put
35          // in the standard place.
36          Configuration config = new Configuration();
37
38          // Tell it about the classes we want mapped, taking advantage of
39          // the way we've named their mapping documents.
40          config.addClass(Track.class);
41
42          // Get the session factory we can use for persistence
43          SessionFactory sessionFactory = config.buildSessionFactory();
44
45          // Ask for a session using the JDBC information we've configured
46          Session session = sessionFactory.openSession();
47          try {
48              // Print the tracks that will fit in five minutes
49              List tracks = tracksNoLongerThan(Time.valueOf("00:05:00"),
50                                                  session);
51              for (ListIterator iter = tracks.listIterator() ;
52                  iter.hasNext() ; ) {
53                  Track aTrack = (Track)iter.next();
```

Example 3-5. *QueryTest.java* (continued)

```
54              System.out.println("Track: \"" + aTrack.getTitle() +
55                                  "\", " + aTrack.getPlayTime());
56            }
57          } finally {
58            // No matter what, close the session
59            session.close();
60          }
61
62          // Clean up after ourselves
63          sessionFactory.close();
64        }
65  }
```

Again, add a target (Example 3-6) at the end of *build.xml* to run this test.

Example 3-6. Ant target to invoke our query test

```
<target name="qtest" description="Run a simple Hibernate query"
        depends="compile">
  <java classname="com.oreilly.hh.QueryTest" fork="true">
    <classpath refid="project.class.path"/>
  </java>
</target>
```

With this in place, we can simply type **ant qtest** to retrieve and display some data, with the results shown in Example 3-7. To save space in the output, we've edited our *log4j.properties* to turn off all the "Info" messages, since they're no different than in the previous example. You can do this yourself by changing the line:

```
log4j.logger.net.sf.hibernate=info
```

to replace the word info with warn:

```
log4j.logger.net.sf.hibernate=warn
```

Example 3-7. Running the query test

```
% ant qtest
Buildfile: build.xml

prepare:

compile:
    [javac] Compiling 1 source file to /Users/jim/Documents/Work/OReilly/
Hibernate/Examples/ch03/classes

qtest:
    [java] Track: "Russian Trance", 00:03:30
    [java] Track: "Video Killed the Radio Star", 00:03:49

BUILD SUCCESSFUL
Total time: 11 seconds
```

What just happened?

If you don't want to deal with any query syntax at all, check out criteria queries in Chapter 8!

In Example 3-5, we started out by defining a utility method, tracksNoLongerThan() on lines 14–28, which performs the actual Hibernate query. It retrieves any tracks whose playing time is less than or equal to the amount specified as a parameter. Hibernate queries are written in HQL (Hibernate Query Language—explored in Chapter 9). This is a SQL-inspired but object-oriented query language with important differences from SQL. HQL is explored in Chapter 9. For now, note that it supports parameter placeholders, much like PreparedStatement in JDBC. And, just like in that environment, using them is preferable to putting together queries through string manipulation. As you'll see below, however, Hibernate offers even better ways of working with queries in Java.

The query itself looks a little strange. It starts with "from" rather than "select *something*" as you might expect. While you can certainly use the more familiar format, and will do so when you want to pull out individual properties from an object in your query, if you want to retrieve entire objects you can use this more abbreviated syntax.

When you're working with pre-existing databases and objects, it's important to realize that HQL queries refer to object properties rather than database table

Also note that the query is expressed in terms of the mapped Java *objects* and *properties* rather than the tables and columns. Since the object being used in the query is in the same package as the mapping document, we don't actually need to use a fully qualified class name like this, but it helps remind readers of the query that it's expressed in terms of objects. Keeping the names consistent is a fairly natural choice, and this will always be the case when you're using Hibernate to generate the schema and the data objects, unless you tell it explictly to use different column names.

Also, in HQL—just as in SQL—you can alias a column or table to another name; in fact, you *must* use aliases to refer to specific JavaBeans properties of mapped classes in your where clauses.

With all that in mind, the meaning of the HQL query "from com.oreilly. hh.Track as track where track.playTime <= ?" breaks down like this:

- We're retrieving instances of our persistent Java data bean Track. (This happens to be stored in the database table called TRACK, but that is managed by the mapping document for class Track; the table could be called anything.) Since we started the query with the from clause (rather than a select clause), we want to obtain entire Track instances as the result of the query.

- Within the query, we are defining an alias "track" to refer to one particular instance of the Track class at a time, so we can specify the properties of the instances we'd like to retrieve.

- The instances we want are those where the playTime property has a value that's less than or equal to the first (and only) query parameter we're passing in at runtime. (Once again, the fact that the playTime property is mapped to the PLAYTIME column is a detail that is buried in the Track mapping document, and it need not be true.)

HQL reads a lot like SQL, but the semantics are different—they refer to the world of the Java program rather than the world of the relational database. This will be more clear in later examples and in Chapter 9 where we perform more complex queries.

The rest of the program should look mighty familiar from the previous example. Our try block is simplified because we don't need a transaction, as we're not changing any data. We still use one so that we can have a finally clause to close our session cleanly. The body is quite simple, calling our query method to request any tracks whose playing time is five minutes or less, and then iterating over the resulting Track objects, printing their titles and playing times.

What about...

...Deleting objects? If you've made changes to your data creation script and want to start with a "clean slate" in the form of an empty database so you can test them, all you need to do is run **ant schema** again. This will drop and recreate the Track table in a pristine and empty state. Don't do it unless you mean it!

If you want to be more selective about what you delete, you can either do it through SQL commands in the HSQLDB UI (**ant db**), or you can make a variant of the query test example that retrieves the objects you want to get rid of. Once you've got a reference to a persistent object, passing it to the Session's delete() method will remove it from the database:

```
session.delete(aTrack);
```

You've still got at least one reference to it in your program, until aTrack goes out of scope or gets reassigned, so conceptually the easiest way to understand what delete() does is to think of it as turning a persistent object back into a transient one.

Another way to use the delete() method is to pass it an HQL query string that matches multiple objects. This lets you delete many persisted objects at once, without writing your own loop. A Java-based alternative to **ant schema**, and a slightly less violent way of clearing out all the tracks, would therefore be something like this:

```
session.delete("from com.oreilly.hh.Track");
```

TIP

Don't forget that regardless of which of these approaches you use, you'll need to wrap the data manipulation code inside a Hibernate transaction, and commit the transaction if you want your changes to "stick."

Better Ways to Build Queries

As mentioned earlier, HQL lets you go beyond the use of JDBC-style query placeholders to get parameters conveniently into your queries. The features discussed in this section can make your programs much easier to read and maintain.

Use named parameters to control queries and move the query text completely outside of your Java source code.

Why do I care?

Well, I've already promised that this will make your programs easier to write, read, and update. In fact, if these features weren't available in Hibernate, I would have been less eager to adopt it, because they've been part of my own (even more) lightweight O/R layer for years.

Named parameters make code easier to understand because the purpose of the parameter is clear both within the query itself and within the Java code that is setting it up. This self-documenting nature is valuable in itself, but it also reduces the potential for error by freeing you from counting commas and question marks, and it can modestly improve efficiency by letting you use the same parameter more than once in a single query.

If you haven't yet had to deal with this, trust me, it's well worth avoiding.

Keeping the queries out of Java source code makes them *much* easier to read and edit because they aren't giant concatenated series of Java strings spread across multiple lines and interleaved with extraneous quotation marks, backslashes, and other Java punctuation. Typing them the first time is bad enough, but if you've ever had to perform significant surgery on a query embedded in a program in this way, you will have had your fill of moving quotation marks and plus signs around to try to get the lines to break in nice places again.

How do I do that?

The key to both of these capabilities in Hibernate is the Query interface. We'll start by changing our query to use a named parameter (Example 3-8). (This isn't nearly as big a deal for a query with a single parameter like this one, but it's worth getting into the habit right away. You'll be very thankful when you start working with the light-dimming queries that power your real projects!)

Example 3-8. Revising our query to use a named parameter

```
public static List tracksNoLongerThan(Time length, Session session)
    throws HibernateException
{
    Query query = session.createQuery("from com.oreilly.hh.Track as track " +
                                      "where track.playTime <= :length");
    query.setTime("length", length);
    return query.list();
}
```

Named parameters are identified within the query body by prefixing them with a colon. Here, we've changed the "?" to ":length". The Session object provides a createQuery() method that gives us back an implementation of the Query interface with which we can work. Query has a full complement of type-safe methods for setting the values of named parameters. Here we are passing in a Time value, so we use setTime(). Even in a simple case like this, the syntax is more natural and readable than the original version of our query. If we had been passing in anonymous arrays of values and types (as would have been necessary with more than one parameter), the improvement would be even more significant. And we've added a layer of compile-time type checking, always a welcome change.

Running this version produces the same output as our original program.

So how do we get the query text out of the Java source? Again, this query is short enough that the need to do so isn't as pressing as usual in real projects, but it's the best way to do things, so let's start practicing! As you may have predicted, the place we can store queries is inside the mapping document. Example 3-9 shows what it looks like (we have to use the somewhat clunky CDATA construct since our query contains characters—like "<"—that could otherwise confuse the XML parser).

Example 3-9. Our query in the mapping document

```
<query name="com.oreilly.hh.tracksNoLongerThan">
  <![CDATA[
      from com.oreilly.hh.Track as track
```

Example 3-9. Our query in the mapping document (continued)

```
        where track.playTime <= :length
    ]]>
</query>
```

Put this just after the closing tag of the class definition in *Track.hbm.xml* (right before the </hibernate-mapping> line). Then we can revise *QueryTest.java* one last time, as shown in Example 3-10. Once again, the program produces exactly the same output as the initial version. It's just better organized now, and we're in great shape if we ever want to make the query more complex.

Example 3-10. The final version of our query method

```
public static List tracksNoLongerThan(Time length, Session session)
    throws HibernateException
{
    Query query = session.getNamedQuery(
                    "com.oreilly.hh.tracksNoLongerThan");
    query.setTime("length", length);
    return query.list();
}
```

The Query interface has other useful capabilities beyond what we've examined here. You can use it to control how many rows (and which specific rows) you retrieve. If your JDBC driver supports scrollable ResultSets, you can access this capability as well. Check the JavaDoc or the Hibernate reference manual for more details.

What about...

...Avoiding a SQL-like language altogether? Or diving in to HQL and exploring more complex queries? These are both options that are covered later in the book.

Chapter 8 discusses criteria queries, an interesting mechanism that lets you express the constraints on the entities you want, using a natural Java API. This gives you the benefits of compile-time syntax checking, and easy dynamic configuration, all in the language you're already using to code your application. It also supports a form of "query by example," where you can supply objects that are similar to the ones you're searching for.

SQL veterans who'd like to see more tricks with HQL can jump to Chapter 9, which explores more of its capabilities and unique features.

For now, we'll continue our examination of mapping by seeing how to represent groups and links between objects.

## CHAPTER 4

Collections and Associations

No, this isn't about taxes or politics. Now that we've seen how easy it is to get individual objects into and out of a database, it's time to see how to work with groups and relationships between objects. Happily, it's no more difficult.

Mapping Collections

In any real application you'll be managing lists and groups of things. Java provides a healthy and useful set of library classes to help with this: the Collections utilities. Hibernate provides natural ways for mapping database relationships onto Collections, which are usually very convenient. You do need to be aware of a couple semantic mismatches, generally minor. The biggest is the fact that Collections don't provide "bag" semantics, which might frustrate some experienced database designers. This gap isn't Hibernate's fault, and it even makes some effort to work around the issue.

Enough abstraction! The Hibernate reference manual does a good job of discussing the whole bag issue, so let's leave it and look at a working example of mapping a collection where the relational and Java models fit nicely. It might seem natural to build on the Track examples from Chapter 3 and group them into albums, but that's not the simplest place to start, because organizing an album involves tracking additional information, like the disc on which the track is found (for multi-disc albums), and other such finicky details. So let's add artist information to our database.

The information we need to keep track of for artists is, at least initially, pretty simple. We'll start with just the artist's name. And each track can be assigned a set of artists, so we know who to thank or blame for the music, and you can look up all tracks by someone we like. (It really is

Bags are like sets, except that the same value can appear more than once.

As usual, the examples assume you followed the steps in the previous chapters. If not, download the example source as a starting point.

critical to allow more than one artist to be assigned to a track, yet so few music management programs get this right. The task of adding a separate link to keep track of composers is left as a useful exercise for the reader after understanding this example.)

How do I do that?

For now, our Artist class doesn't need anything other than a name property (and its key, of course). Setting up a mapping document for it will be easy. Create the file *Artist.hbm.xml* in the same directory as the Track mapping document, with the contents shown in Example 4-1.

Example 4-1. Mapping document for the Artist class

```
1  <?xml version="1.0"?>
2  <!DOCTYPE hibernate-mapping PUBLIC "-//Hibernate/Hibernate Mapping DTD 2.0//EN"
3          "http://hibernate.sourceforge.net/hibernate-mapping-2.0.dtd">
4
5  <hibernate-mapping>
6
7    <class name="com.oreilly.hh.Artist" table="ARTIST">
8      <meta attribute="class-description">
9        Represents an artist who is associated with a track or album.
10       @author Jim Elliott (with help from Hibernate)
11     </meta>
12
13     <id name="id" type="int" column="ARTIST_ID">
14       <meta attribute="scope-set">protected</meta>
15       <generator class="native"/>
16     </id>
17
18     <property name="name" type="string">
19       <meta attribute="use-in-tostring">true</meta>
20       <column name="NAME" not-null="true" unique="true" index="ARTIST_NAME"/>
21     </property>
22
23     <set name="tracks" table="TRACK_ARTISTS" inverse="true">
24       <meta attribute="field-description">Tracks by this artist</meta>
25       <key column="ARTIST_ID"/>
26       <many-to-many class="com.oreilly.hh.Track" column="TRACK_ID"/>
27     </set>
28
29   </class>
30
31  </hibernate-mapping>
```

Our mapping for the name property on lines 18–21 introduces a couple of refinements to both the code generation and schema generation phases. The use-in-tostring meta tag causes the generated class to show the artist's name as well as the cryptic synthetic ID when it is printed, as an aid for debugging (you can see the result near the bottom of Example 4-3). And expanding the column attribute into a full-blown tag allows us finer-grained control over the nature of the column, which we use in this case to add an index for efficient lookup and sorting by name.

Notice that we can represent the fact that an artist is associated with one or more tracks quite naturally in this file (lines 23–27). This tells Hibernate to add a property named tracks to our Artist class, whose type is an implementation of java.util.Set. This will use a new table named TRACK_ARTISTS to link to the Track objects for which this Artist is responsible. The attribute inverse="true" is explained in the discussion of Example 4-2, where the bidirectional nature of this association is examined.

The TRACK_ARTISTS table we just called into existence will contain two columns: TRACK_ID and ARTIST_ID. Any rows appearing in this table will mean that the specified Artist object has something to do with the specified Track object. The fact that this information lives in its own table means that there is no restriction on how many tracks can be linked to a particular artist, nor how many artists are associated with a track. That's what is meant by a "many-to-many" association.*

On the flip side, since these links are in a separate table you have to perform a join query in order to retrieve any meaningful information about either the artists or the tracks. This is why such tables are often called "join tables." Their whole purpose is to be used to join other tables together.

Finally, notice that unlike the other tables we've set up in our schema, TRACK_ARTISTS does not correspond to any mapped Java object. It is used only to implement the links between Artist and Track objects, as reflected by Artist's tracks property.

As seen on line 24, the field-description meta tag can be used to provide JavaDoc descriptions for collections and associations as well as plain old value fields. This is handy in situations where the field name isn't completely self-documenting.

The tweaks and configuration choices provided by the mapping document, especially when aided by meta tags, give you a great deal of

---

* If concepts like join tables and many-to-many associations aren't familiar, spending some time with a good data modeling introduction would be worthwhile. It will help a lot when it comes to designing, understanding, and talking about data-driven projects. George Reese's *Java Database Best Practices* (O'Reilly) has one, and you can even view this chapter online at *http://www.oreilly.com/catalog/javadtabp/chapter/ch02.pdf*.

flexibility over how the source code and database schema are built. Nothing can quite compare to the control you can obtain by writing them yourself, but most common needs and scenarios appear to be within reach of the mapping-driven generation tools. This is great news, because they can save you a lot of tedious typing!

With that in place, let's add the collection of Artists to our Track class. Edit *Track.hbm.xml* to include the new artists property as shown in Example 4-2 (the new content is shown in bold).

Example 4-2. Adding an artist collection to the Track mapping file

```
...
<property name="playTime" type="time">
  <meta attribute="field-description">Playing time</meta>
</property>

<set name="artists" table="TRACK_ARTISTS">
  <key column="TRACK_ID"/>
  <many-to-many class="com.oreilly.hh.Artist" column="ARTIST_ID"/>
</set>

<property name="added" type="date">
  <meta attribute="field-description">When the track was created</meta>
</property>
...
```

This adds a similar Set property named artists to the Track class. It uses the same TRACK_ARTISTS join table introduced in Example 4-1 to link to the Artist objects we mapped there. This sort of bidirectional association is very useful. It's important to let hibernate know explicitly what's going on by marking one end of the association as "inverse." In the case of a many-to-many association like this one, the choice of which side to call the inverse mapping isn't crucial. The fact that the join table is named "track artists" makes the link from artists back to tracks the best choice for the inverse end, if only from the perspective of people trying to understand the database. Hibernate itself doesn't care, as long as we mark one of the directions as inverse. That's why we did so on line 23 of Example 4-1.

While we're updating the Track mapping document we might as well beef up the title property along the lines of what we did for name in Artist:

```
<property name="title" type="string">
  <meta attribute="use-in-tostring">true</meta>
  <column name="TITLE" not-null="true" index="TRACK_TITLE"/>
</property>
```

With the new and updated mapping files in place, we're ready to rerun **ant codegen** to update the Track source code, and create the new Artist source. This time Hibernate reports that two files are processed, as expected. If you look at *Track.java* you'll see the new Set-valued property artists has been added, and toString() has been enhanced. Example 4-3 shows the content of the new *Artist.java*.

Example 4-3. Code generated for the Artist class

```java
package com.oreilly.hh;

import java.io.Serializable;
import java.util.Set;
import org.apache.commons.lang.builder.EqualsBuilder;
import org.apache.commons.lang.builder.HashCodeBuilder;
import org.apache.commons.lang.builder.ToStringBuilder;

/**
 *         Represents an artist who is associated with a track or album.
 *         @author Jim Elliott (with help from Hibernate)
 *
 */
public class Artist implements Serializable {

    /** identifier field */
    private Integer id;

    /** nullable persistent field */
    private String name;

    /** persistent field */
    private Set tracks;

    /** full constructor */
    public Artist(String name, Set tracks) {
        this.name = name;
        this.tracks = tracks;
    }

    /** default constructor */
    public Artist() {
    }

    /** minimal constructor */
    public Artist(Set tracks) {
        this.tracks = tracks;
    }

    public Integer getId() {
        return this.id;
    }
```

Example 4-3. Code generated for the Artist class (continued)

```java
    protected void setId(Integer id) {
        this.id = id;
    }

    public String getName() {
        return this.name;
    }

    public void setName(String name) {
        this.name = name;
    }

    /**
     * Tracks by this artist
     */
    public Set getTracks() {
        return this.tracks;
    }

    public void setTracks(Set tracks) {
        this.tracks = tracks;
    }

    public String toString() {
        return new ToStringBuilder(this)
            .append("id", getId())
            .append("name", getName())
            .toString();
    }

    public boolean equals(Object other) {
        if ( !(other instanceof Artist) ) return false;
        Artist castOther = (Artist) other;
        return new EqualsBuilder()
            .append(this.getId(), castOther.getId())
            .isEquals();
    }

    public int hashCode() {
        return new HashCodeBuilder()
            .append(getId())
            .toHashCode();
    }

}
```

Once the classes are created, we can use **ant schema** to build the new database schema that supports them.

The generated schema contains the tables we'd expect, along with indices and some clever foreign key constraints. As our object model gets more sophisticated, the amount of work (and expertise) being provided by Hibernate is growing nicely. The full output from the schema generation is rather long, but Example 4-4 shows highlights.

Example 4-4. Excerpts from our new schema generation

```
[schemaexport] create table TRACK_ARTISTS (
[schemaexport]     ARTIST_ID INTEGER not null,
[schemaexport]     TRACK_ID INTEGER not null,
[schemaexport]     primary key (TRACK_ID, ARTIST_ID)
[schemaexport] )
...
[schemaexport] create table ARTIST (
[schemaexport]     ARTSIT_ID INTEGER NOT NULL IDENTITY,
[schemaexport]     name VARCHAR(255) not null,
[schemaexport]     unique (name)
[schemaexport] )
...
[schemaexport] create table TRACK (
[schemaexport]     Track_id INTEGER NOT NULL IDENTITY,
[schemaexport]     title VARCHAR(255) not null,
[schemaexport]     filePath VARCHAR(255) not null,
[schemaexport]     playTime TIME,
[schemaexport]     added DATE,
[schemaexport]     volume SMALLINT
[schemaexport] )
...
[schemaexport] alter table TRACK_ARTISTS add constraint FK72EFDAD84C5F92B foreign
key (TRACK_ID) references TRACK
[schemaexport] alter table TRACK_ARTISTS add constraint FK72EFDAD87395D347
foreign key (ARTIST_ID) references ARTIST
[schemaexport] create index ARTIST_NAME on ARTIST (name)
[schemaexport] create index TRACK_TITLE on TRACK (title))
```

Cool! I didn't even know how to do some of that stuff in HSQLDB!

Figure 4-1 shows HSQLDB's tree view representation of the schema after these additions. I'm not sure why two separate indices are used to set up the uniqueness constraint on artist names, but that seems to be an implementation quirk in HSQLDB itself, and this approach will work just fine.

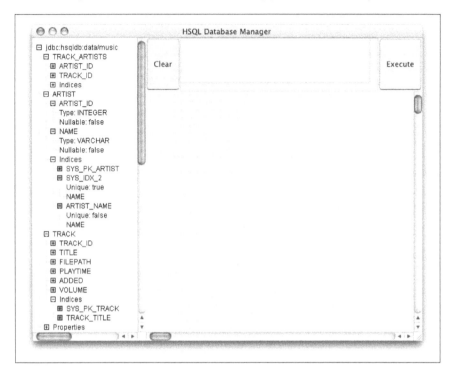

Figure 4-1. The HSQLDB graphical tree view of our updated schema

What just happened?

We've set up an object model that allows our Track and Artist objects to keep track of an arbitrary set of relationships to each other. Any track can be associated with any number of artists, and any artist can be responsible for any number of tracks. Getting this set up right can be challenging, especially for people who are new to object-oriented code or relational databases (or both!), so it's nice to have Hibernate help. But just wait until you see how easy it is to work with data in this setup.

It's worth emphasizing that the links between artists and tracks are not stored in the ARTIST or TRACK tables themselves. Because they are in a many-to-many association, meaning that an artist can be associated with many tracks, and many artists can be associated with a track, these links are stored in a separate join table called TRACK_ARTISTS. Rows in this table pair an ARTIST_ID with a TRACK_ID, to indicate that the specified artist is associated with the specified track. By creating and deleting rows in this table, we can set up any pattern of associations we need. (This is how many-to-many relationships are always represented in relational databases; the chapter of *Java Database Best Practices* cited earlier is a good introduction to data models like this.)

Keeping this in mind, you will also notice that our generated classes don't contain any code to manage the TRACK_ARTISTS table. Nor will the upcoming examples that create and link persistent Track and Artist objects. They don't have to, because Hibernate's special Collection classes take care of all those details for us, based on the mapping information we added to Example 4-2 and lines 23–27 of Example 4-1.

All right, let's create some tracks and artists....

Note to self: time to start selling co-workers on this Hibernate stuff!

Persisting Collections

Our first task is to beef up the CreateTest class to take advantage of the new richness in our schema, creating some artists and associating them with tracks.

How do I do that?

To begin with, add some helper methods to *CreateTest.java* to simplify the task, as shown in Example 4-5 (with changes and additions in bold).

Example 4-5. Utility methods to help find and create artists, and to link them to tracks

```
1   package com.oreilly.hh;
2
3   import net.sf.hibernate.*;
4
5   import net.sf.hibernate.cfg.Configuration;
6
7   import java.sql.Time;
8   import java.util.*;
9
10  /**
11   * Create more sample data, letting Hibernate persist it for us.
12   */
13  public class CreateTest {
14
15      /**
16       * Look up an artist record given a name.
17       * @param name the name of the artist desired.
18       * @param create controls whether a new record should be created if
```

```
19        *        the specified artist is not yet in the database.
20        * @param session the Hibernate session that can retrieve data
21        * @return the artist with the specified name, or <code>null</code> if no
22        * such artist exists and <code>create</code> is <code>false</code>.
23        * @throws HibernateException if there is a problem.
24        */
25       public static Artist getArtist(String name, boolean create,
26                                       Session session)
27           throws HibernateException
28       {
29           Query query = session.getNamedQuery(
30                           "com.oreilly.hh.artistByName");
31           query.setString("name", name);
32           Artist found = (Artist)query.uniqueResult();
33           if (found == null && create) {
34               found = new Artist(name, new HashSet());
35               session.save(found);
36           }
37           return found;
38       }
39
40       /**
41        * Utility method to associate an artist with a track
42        */
43       private static void addTrackArtist(Track track, Artist artist) {
44           track.getArtists().add(artist);
45       }
```

As is so often the case when working with Hibernate, this code is pretty simple and self explanatory. (Do notice that line 8 has changed—we used to import java.util.Date, but we're now importing the whole util package to work with Collections. The "*" is bold to highlight this, but it's easy to miss when scanning the example.)

We'll want to reuse the same artists if we create multiple tracks for them— that's the whole point of using an Artist object rather than just storing strings—so our getArtist() method (starting at line 15) does the work of looking them up by name. The uniqueResult() method it uses on line 32 is a convenience feature of the Query interface, perfect in situations like this, where we know we'll either get one result or none. It saves us the trouble of getting back a list of results, checking the length and extracting the first result if it's there. We'll either get back the single result or null if there were none. (We'd be thrown an exception if there were more than one result, but our unique constraint on the column will prevent that.)

So all we need to do is check for null on line 33, and create a new Artist (lines 34–35) if we didn't find one and we're supposed to.

The `addTrackArtist()` method (lines 40–45) is almost embarrassingly
simple. It's just ordinary Java `Collections` code that grabs the `Set` of artists belonging to a `Track` and adds the specified `Artist` to it. Can that
really do everything we need? Where's all the database manipulation
code we normally have to write? Welcome to the wonderful world of
objectrelational mapping tools!

You might have noticed that `getArtist()` uses a named query to retrieve
the `Artist` record. In Example 4-6, we will add that at the end of
`Artist.hbm.xml` (actually, we could put it in any mapping file, but this is
the most sensible place, since it relates to `Artist` records).

Example 4-6. Artist lookup query to be added to the artist mapping document

```
<query name="com.oreilly.hh.artistByName">
  <![CDATA[
     from com.oreilly.hh.Artist as artist
     where upper(artist.name) = upper(:name)
  ]]>
</query>
```

We use the `upper()` function to perform case-insensitive comparison of artists' names, so that we retrieve the artist even if the capitalization is different during lookup than what's stored in the database. This sort of case-
insensitive but preserving architecture, a user-friendly concession to the
way humans like to work, is worth implementing whenever possible. Databases other than HSQLDB may have a different name for the function that
converts strings to uppercase, but there should be one available.

Now we can use this infrastructure to actually create some tracks with
linked artists. Example 4-7 shows the remainder of the `CreateTest` class
with the additions marked in bold. Edit your copy to match (or download
it to save the typing).

Example 4-7. Revisions to main method of *CreateTest.java* in order to add artist
associations

```
1  public static void main(String args[]) throws Exception {
2      // Create a configuration based on the properties file we've put
3      // in the standard place.
```

Example 4-7. *Revisions to main method of CreateTest.java in order to add artist associations (continued)*

```
4       Configuration config = new Configuration();
5
6       // Tell it about the classes we want mapped, taking advantage of
7       // the way we've named their mapping documents.
8       config.addClass(Track.class).addClass(Artist.class);
9
10      // Get the session factory we can use for persistence
11      SessionFactory sessionFactory = config.buildSessionFactory();
12
13      // Ask for a session using the JDBC information we've configured
14      Session session = sessionFactory.openSession();
15      Transaction tx = null;
16      try {
17          // Create some data and persist it
18          tx = session.beginTransaction();
19
20          Track track = new Track("Russian Trance",
21                                  "vol2/album610/track02.mp3",
22                                  Time.valueOf("00:03:30"), new Date(),
23                                  (short)0, new HashSet());
24          addTrackArtist(track, getArtist("PPK", true, session));
25          session.save(track);
26
27          track = new Track("Video Killed the Radio Star",
28                                  "vol2/album611/track12.mp3",
29                                  Time.valueOf("00:03:49"), new Date(),
30                                  (short)0, new HashSet());
31          addTrackArtist(track, getArtist("The Buggles", true, session));
32          session.save(track);
33
34
35          track = new Track("Gravity's Angel",
36                                  "vol2/album175/track03.mp3",
37                                  Time.valueOf("00:06:06"), new Date(),
38                                  (short)0, new HashSet());
39          addTrackArtist(track, getArtist("Laurie Anderson", true, session));
40          session.save(track);
41
42          track = new Track("Adagio for Strings (Ferry Corsten Remix)",
43                                  "vol2/album972/track01.mp3",
44                                  Time.valueOf("00:06:35"), new Date(),
45                                  (short)0, new HashSet());
46          addTrackArtist(track, getArtist("William Orbit", true, session));
47          addTrackArtist(track, getArtist("Ferry Corsten", true, session));
48          addTrackArtist(track, getArtist("Samuel Barber", true, session));
49          session.save(track);
50
51          track = new Track("Adagio for Strings (ATB Remix)",
52                                  "vol2/album972/track02.mp3",
53                                  Time.valueOf("00:07:39"), new Date(),
54                                  (short)0, new HashSet());
```

```
55          addTrackArtist(track, getArtist("William Orbit", true, session));
56          addTrackArtist(track, getArtist("ATB", true, session));
57          addTrackArtist(track, getArtist("Samuel Barber", true, session));
58          session.save(track);
59
60          track = new Track("The World '99",
61                              "vol2/singles/pvw99.mp3",
62                              Time.valueOf("00:07:05"), new Date(),
63                              (short)0, new HashSet());
64          addTrackArtist(track, getArtist("Pulp Victim", true, session));
65          addTrackArtist(track, getArtist("Ferry Corsten", true, session));
66          session.save(track);
67
68          track = new Track("Test Tone 1",
69                              "vol2/singles/test01.mp3",
70                              Time.valueOf("00:00:10"), new Date(),
71                              (short)0, new HashSet());
72          session.save(track);
73
74          // We're done; make our changes permanent
75          tx.commit();
76
77      } catch (Exception e) {
78          if (tx != null) {
79              // Something went wrong; discard all partial changes
80              tx.rollback();
81          }
82          throw e;
83      } finally {
84          // No matter what, close the session
85          session.close();
86      }
87
88      // Clean up after ourselves
89      sessionFactory.close();
90  }
91 }
```

The changes to the existing code are pretty minimal. First we need to
map our new Artist class, which takes just one method call on line 8
(again, thanks to the naming convention we've been following to link our
mapping documents to their classes). The lines that created the three
tracks from Chapter 3 need only a single new parameter each, to supply
an initially empty set of Artist associations (lines 23, 30, and 38). Each
also gets a new follow-up line establishing an association to the artist for
that track. We could have structured this code differently, by writing a
helper method to create the initial HashSet containing the artist, so we
could do this all in one line. The approach we actually used scales better
to multi-artist tracks, as the next section illustrates.

The largest chunk of new code, lines 42–66, simply adds three new tracks to show how multiple artists per track are handled. If you like electronica and dance remixes (or classical for that matter), you know how important an issue that can be. Because we set the links up as collections, it's simply a matter of adding each artist link to the tracks. Finally, lines 68–72 add a track with no artist associations to see how that behaves, too. Now you can run **ant ctest** to create the new sample data containing tracks, artists, and associations between them.

Of course, in real life you'd be setting this data into the database in some other way— through a user interface, or as part of the process of importing the actual music.

TIP

A useful trick if you're making changes to your test data creation program and you want to try it again starting from an empty database is to issue the command **ant schema ctest**. This tells Ant to run the schema and ctest targets one after the other. Running schema blows away any existing data; then ctest gets to create it anew.

What just happened?

There's no visible output from running ctest: look at *data/music.script* to see what got created or fire up **ant db** to look at it via the graphical interface. Take a look at the contents of the three tables. Figure 4-2 shows what ended up in the join table that represents associations between artists and tracks. The raw data is becoming cryptic. If you're used to relational modeling, this query shows you everything worked. If you're mortal like me, the next section is more convincing; it's certainly more fun.

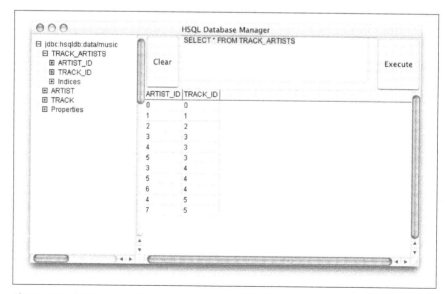

Figure 4-2. Artist and track associations created by the new version of CreateTest

Retrieving Collections

You might expect that getting the collection information back out of the database is similarly easy. You'd be right! Let's enhance our QueryTest class to show us the artists associated with the tracks it displays. Example 4-8 shows the appropriate changes and additions in bold. Little new code is needed.

Example 4-8. *QueryTest.java* enhanced in order to display artists associated with tracks

```
1   package com.oreilly.hh;
2
3   import net.sf.hibernate.*;
4   import net.sf.hibernate.cfg.Configuration;
5
6   import java.sql.Time;
7   import java.util.*;
8
9   /**
10   * Retrieve data as objects
11   */
12  public class QueryTest {
13
14      /**
15       * Retrieve any tracks that fit in the specified amount of time.
16       *
17       * @param length the maximum playing time for tracks to be returned.
18       * @param session the Hibernate session that can retrieve data.
19       * @return a list of {@link Track}s meeting the length restriction.
20       * @throws HibernateException if there is a problem.
21       */
22      public static List tracksNoLongerThan(Time length, Session session)
23          throws HibernateException
24      {
25          Query query = session.getNamedQuery(
26                          "com.oreilly.hh.tracksNoLongerThan");
27          query.setTime("length", length);
28          return query.list();
29      }
30
31      /**
32       * Build a parenthetical, comma-separated list of artist names.
33       * @param artists the artists whose names are to be displayed.
34       * @return formatted list, or an empty string if the set was empty.
35       */
36      public static String listArtistNames(Set artists) {
37          StringBuffer result = new StringBuffer();
38          for (Iterator iter = artists.iterator(); iter.hasNext(); ) {
39              Artist artist = (Artist)iter.next();
40              result.append((result.length() == 0) ? "(" : ", ");
41              result.append(artist.getName());
```

Example 4-8. *QueryTest.java* enhanced in order to display artists associated with tracks (continued)

```
42              }
43              if (result.length() > 0) {
44                  result.append(") ");
45              }
46              return result.toString();
47          }
48
49          /**
50           * Look up and print some tracks when invoked from the command line.
51           */
52          public static void main(String args[]) throws Exception {
53              // Create a configuration based on the properties file we've put
54              // in the standard place.
55              Configuration config = new Configuration();
56
57              // Tell it about the classes we want mapped, taking advantage of
58              // the way we've named their mapping documents.
59              config.addClass(Track.class).addClass(Artist.class);
60
61              // Get the session factory we can use for persistence
62              SessionFactory sessionFactory = config.buildSessionFactory();
63
64              // Ask for a session using the JDBC information we've configured
65              Session session = sessionFactory.openSession();
66              try {
67                  // Print the tracks that will fit in seven minutes
68                  List tracks = tracksNoLongerThan(Time.valueOf("00:07:00"),
69                                  session);
70                  for (ListIterator iter = tracks.listIterator() ;
71                      iter.hasNext() ; ) {
72                      Track aTrack = (Track)iter.next();
73                      System.out.println("Track: \"" + aTrack.getTitle() + "\" " +
74                                  listArtistNames(aTrack.getArtists()) +
75                                  aTrack.getPlayTime());
76                  }
77              } finally {
78                  // No matter what, close the session
79                  session.close();
80              }
81
82              // Clean up after ourselves
83              sessionFactory.close();
84          }
85      }
```

How easy was that?

The first thing we add is a little utility method (lines 31–47) to format the set of artist names nicely, as a comma-delimited list inside parentheses, with proper spacing, or as nothing at all if the set of artists is empty.

Next, as with `CreateTest`, we need to tell Hibernate to map our new Artist class on line 59. Since all the interesting new multi-artist tracks are longer than five minutes, we increase the cutoff in our query to seven minutes so we can see some (line 68). Finally we call `listArtistNames()` at the proper position in the `println()` statement describing the tracks found (line 74).

Example 4-9 shows the new output from **ant qtest**.

Example 4-9. *QueryTest* output with artist information

```
% ant qtest
Buildfile: build.xml

prepare:

compile:
    [javac] Compiling 1 source file to /Users/jim/Documents/Work/OReilly/
Hibernate/Examples/ch04/classes

qtest:
    [java] Track: "Russian Trance" (PPK) 00:03:30
    [java] Track: "Video Killed the Radio Star" (The Buggles) 00:03:49
    [java] Track: "Gravity's Angel" (Laurie Anderson) 00:06:06
    [java] Track: "Adagio for Strings (Ferry Corsten Remix)" (Ferry Corsten,
William Orbit, Samuel Barber) 00:06:35
    [java] Track: "Test Tone 1" 00:00:10

BUILD SUCCESSFUL
Total time: 17 seconds
11.940u 1.510s 0:18.06 74.4%    0+0k 0+7io 0pf+0w
```

You'll notice two things. First, that this is much easier to interpret than the columns of numbers in Figure 4-2. And second, it worked! Even in the "tricky" case of the test tone track without any artist mappings, Hibernate takes the friendly approach of creating an empty artists Set, sparing us from peppering our code with the null checks we'd otherwise need to avoid crashing with NullPointerExceptions.

But wait, there's more! No additional code needed...

Using Bidirectional Associations

In our creation code, we established links from tracks to artists, simply by adding Java objects to appropriate collections. Hibernate did the work of translating these associations and groupings into the necessary cryptic entries in a join table it created for that purpose. It allowed us with easy, readable code to establish and probe these relationships. But remember that we made this association bidirectional—the Artist class has a collection of Track associations too. We didn't bother to store anything in there.

The great news is that we don't have to. Because of the fact that we marked this as an inverse mapping in the Artist mapping document, Hibernate understands that when we add an Artist association to a Track, we're implicitly adding that Track as an association to the Artist at the same time.

WARNING

This convenience works only when you make changes to the "primary" mapping, in which case they propagate to the inverse mapping. If you make changes only to the inverse mapping, in our case the Set of tracks in the Artist object, they will not be persisted. This unfortunately means your code must be sensitive to which mapping is the inverse.

Let's build a simple interactive graphical application that can help us check whether the artist to track links really show up. It will let you type in an artist's name, and show you all the tracks associated with that artist. A lot of the code is very similar to our first query test. Create the file *QueryTest2.java* and enter the code shown in Example 4-10.

Example 4-10. Source for *QueryTest2.java*

```
1   package com.oreilly.hh;
2
3   import net.sf.hibernate.*;
4   import net.sf.hibernate.cfg.Configuration;
5
6   import java.sql.Time;
7   import java.util.*;
8   import java.awt.*;
9   import java.awt.event.*;
10  import javax.swing.*;
11
12  /**
13   * Provide a user interface to enter artist names and see their tracks.
14   */
15  public class QueryTest2 extends JPanel {
16
17      JList list;  // Will contain tracks associated with current artist
18      DefaultListModel model; // Lets us manipulate the list contents
19
20      /**
21       * Build the panel containing UI elements
22       */
23      public QueryTest2() {
24          setLayout(new BorderLayout());
25          model = new DefaultListModel();
26          list = new JList(model);
```

Example 4-10. *Source for QueryTest2.java (continued)*

```
27              add(new JScrollPane(list), BorderLayout.SOUTH);
28
29              final JTextField artistField = new JTextField(30);
30              artistField.addKeyListener(new KeyAdapter() {
31                      public void keyTyped(KeyEvent e) {
32                          SwingUtilities.invokeLater(new Runnable() {
33                              public void run() {
34                                  updateTracks(artistField.getText());
35                              }
36                          });
37                      }
38              });
39              add(artistField, BorderLayout.EAST);
40              add(new JLabel("Artist: "), BorderLayout.WEST);
41          }
42
43          /**
44           * Update the list to contain the tracks associated with an artist
45           */
46          private void updateTracks(String name) {
47              model.removeAllElements();  // Clear out previous tracks
48              if (name.length() < 1) return;    // Nothing to do
49              try {
50                  // Ask for a session using the JDBC information we've configured
51                  Session session = sessionFactory.openSession();
52                  try {
53                      Artist artist = CreateTest.getArtist(name, false, session);
54                      if (artist == null) {  // Unknown artist
55                          model.addElement("Artist not found");
56                          return;
57                      }
58                      // List the tracks associated with the artist
59                      for (Iterator iter = artist.getTracks().iterator() ;
60                           iter.hasNext() ; ) {
61                          Track aTrack = (Track)iter.next();
62                          model.addElement("Track: \"" + aTrack.getTitle() +
63                                          "\", " + aTrack.getPlayTime());
64                      }
65                  } finally {
66                      // No matter what, close the session
67                      session.close();
68                  }
69              } catch (Exception e) {
70                  System.err.println("Problem updating tracks:" + e);
71                  e.printStackTrace();
72              }
73          }
74
75          private static SessionFactory sessionFactory; // Used to talk to Hibernate
76
77          /**
78           * Set up Hibernate, then build and display the user interface.
79           */
```

Example 4-10. *Source for QueryTest2.java* (continued)

```
80      public static void main(String args[]) throws Exception {
81          // Load configuration properties, read mappings for persistent classes.
82          Configuration config = new Configuration();
83          config.addClass(Track.class).addClass(Artist.class);
84
85          // Get the session factory we can use for persistence
86          sessionFactory = config.buildSessionFactory();
87
88          // Set up the UI
89          JFrame frame = new JFrame("Artist Track Lookup");
90          frame.setDefaultCloseOperation(JFrame.EXIT_ON_CLOSE);
91          frame.setContentPane(new QueryTest2());
92          frame.setSize(400, 180);
93          frame.setVisible(true);
94      }
95  }
```

The bulk of the novel code in this example deals with setting up a Swing user interface. It's actually a rather primitive interface, and won't resize nicely, but dealing with such details would make the code larger, and really falls outside the scope of this book. If you want examples of how to build rich, quality Swing interfaces, check out our *Java Swing*, Second Edition (O'Reilly). It's much thicker so it has room for all that good stuff.

Yes, this is a shameless plug.

The only item I want to highlight in the constructor is the KeyListener that gets added to artistField (lines 30–38). This rather tricky bit of code creates an anonymous class whose keyTyped() method is invoked whenever the user types in the artist text field. That method, lines 31–37, tries to update the track display by checking whether the field now contains a recognized artist name. Unfortunately, at the time the method gets invoked, the text field has not yet been updated to reflect the latest keystroke, so we're forced to defer the actual display update to a second anonymous class (the Runnable instance created on lines 32–36) via the invokeLater() method of SwingUtilities. This technique causes the update to happen when Swing "gets around to it," which in our case means the text field will have finished updating itself.

The updateTracks() method that gets called at that point is where the interesting Hibernate stuff happens. It starts by clearing the list on line 47, discarding any tracks it might have previously been displaying. If the artist name is empty, that's all it does. Otherwise, it opens a Hibernate session on line 51 and tries to look up the artist using the getArtist() method we wrote in CreateTest. This time we tell it *not* to create an artist if it can't find the one we asked for, so we'll get back a null if the user hasn't typed the name of a known artist. If that's the case, we just display a message to that effect (line 55).

If we do find an `Artist` record, on the other hand, line 59 iterates over any `Track` records found in the artist's set of associated tracks, and lines 61–63 display information about each one. All this will test whether the inverse association has worked the way we'd like it to. Finally (no pun intended), lines 65–68 make sure to close the session when we're leaving the method, even through an exception. You don't want to leak sessions—that's a good way to bog down and crash your whole database environment.

The `main()` method starts out with the same Hibernate configuration steps we've seen before in lines 81–86, then creates and displays the user interface frame in lines 89–93. Line 90 sets the interface up to end the program when it's closed. After displaying the frame, `main()` returns. From that point on, the Swing event loop is in control.

Once you've created (or downloaded) this source file, you also need to add a new target, shown in Example 4-11, to the end of *build.xml* (the Ant build file) to invoke this new class.

Example 4-11. Ant target for running the new query test

```
<target name="qtest2" description="Run a simple Artist exploration GUI"
        depends="compile">
  <java classname="com.oreilly.hh.QueryTest2" fork="true">
    <classpath refid="project.class.path"/>
  </java>
</target>
```

Now you can fire it up by typing **ant qtest2** and play with it for yourself. Figure 4-3 shows the program in action, displaying tracks for one of the artists in our sample data.

This is very similar to the existing "qtest" target; copy and tweak that.

Figure 4-3. A simple artist tracks browser

Working with Simple Collections

The collections we've been looking at so far have all contained associations to other objects, which is appropriate for a chapter titled "Collections and Associations," but isn't the only kind you can use with Hibernate. You can also define mappings for collections of simple values, like strings, numbers, and nonpersistent value classes.

How do I do that?

Suppose we want to be able to record some number of comments about each track in the database. We want a new property called comments to contain the String values of each associated comment. The new mapping in *Tracks.hbm.xml* looks a lot like what we did for artists, only a bit simpler:

```
<set name="comments" table="TRACK_COMMENTS">
  <key column="TRACK_ID"/>
  <element column="COMMENT" type="string"/>
</set>
```

Since we're able to store an arbitrary number of comments for each Track, we're going to need a new table to put them in. Each comment will be linked to the proper Track through the track's id property.

Rebuilding the databases with **ant schema** shows how this gets built in the database:

```
[schemaexport] create table TRACK_COMMENTS (
[schemaexport]     TRACK_ID INTEGER not null,
[schemaexport]     COMMENT VARCHAR(255)
[schemaexport] )
[schemaexport] alter table TRACK_COMMENTS add constraint FK105B26884C5F92B
foreign key (TRACK_ID) references TRACK
```

Data modeling junkies will recognize this as a "one-to-many" relationship.

After updating the Track class via **ant codegen**, we need to add another Set at the end of each constructor invocation in *CreateTest.java*, for the comments. For example:

```
track = new Track("Test Tone 1",
                  "vol2/singles/test01.mp3",
                  Time.valueOf("00:00:10"), new Date(),
                  (short)0, new HashSet(), new HashSet());
```

Then we can assign a comment on the following line:

```
track.getComments().add("Pink noise to test equalization");
```

A quick **ant ctest** will compile and run this (making sure you've not forgotten to add the second HashSet to any tracks), and you can check *data/music.script* to see how it's stored in the database. Or add another loop after the track `println()` in *QueryTest.java* to print the comments for the track that was just displayed:

```
for (Iterator comIter = aTrack.getComments().iterator() ;
     comIter.hasNext() ; ) {
  System.out.println("  Comment: " + comIter.next());
}
```

Then **ant qtest** will give you output like this:

```
...
[java] Track: "Test Tone 1" 00:00:10
[java]   Comment: Pink noise to test equalization
```

It's nice when tools make simple things easier. In the next chapter we'll see that more complex things are possible too.

Richer Associations

Yes, wealthy friends would be nice. But I can't propose an easy way to get any, so let's look at relationships between objects that carry more information than simple grouping. In this chapter we'll look at the tracks that make up an album. We had put that off in Chapter 4 because organizing an album involves more than simply grouping some tracks; you also need to know the order in which the tracks occur, as well as things like which disc they're on, in order to support multi-disc albums. That goes beyond what you can achieve with an automatically generated join table, so we'll design our own AlbumTrack object and table, and let albums link to these.

Before diving in, there's an important concept called "laziness" we need to explore.

Using Lazy Associations

First rich, then lazy? I suppose that could be a plausible story about someone, as long as it happened in that order. But this really is an object relational mapping topic of some importance. As your data model grows, adding associations between objects and tables, your program gains power, which is great. But you often end up with a large fraction of your objects somehow linked to each other. So what happens when you load one of the objects that is part of a huge interrelated cluster? Since, as you've seen, you can move from one object to its associated objects just by traversing properties, it seems you'd have to load all the associated objects when you load any of them. For small databases this is fine, but in general your database can't hold a lot more than the memory available to your program. Uh oh! And even if it does all fit, rarely will you actually access most of those objects, so it's a waste to load them all.

Luckily, this problem was anticipated by the designers of object/relational mapping software, including Hibernate. The trick is to configure some associations to be "lazy," so that associated objects aren't loaded until they're actually referenced. Hibernate will instead make a note of the linked object's identity and put off loading it until you actually try to access it. This is often done for collections like those we've been using.

How do I do that?

With collections, all you need to do is set the `lazy` attribute in the mapping declaration. For example, our track artists mapping could look like Example 5-1.

Example 5-1. Lazily initializing the track artist associations

```
<set name="artists" table="TRACK_ARTISTS" lazy="true">
  <key column="TRACK"/>
  <many-to-many class="com.oreilly.hh.Artist" column="ARTIST"/>
</set>
```

This would tell Hibernate to use a special lazy implementation of Set that doesn't load its contents from the database until you actually try to use them. This is done completely transparently, so you don't even notice it's taking place in your code.

Well, if it's that simple, and avoids problems with loading giant snarls of interrelated objects, why not do it all the time? The problem is that the transparency breaks down once you've closed your Hibernate session. At that point, if you try to access content from a lazy collection that hasn't been initialized (even if you've assigned the collection to a different variable, or returned it from a method call), the Hibernate-provided proxy collection can no longer access the database to perform the deferred loading of its contents, and it is forced to throw a LazyInitializationException.

Because this can lead to unexpected crashes far away from the Hibernate-specific code, lazy initialization is turned off by default. It's your responsibility to think carefully about situations in which you need to use it, and ensure that you are doing so safely. The Hibernate reference manual goes into a bit of detail about strategies to consider.

Conservation of complexity seems almost like a law of thermodynamics.

What about...

...Laziness outside of collections? Caching and clustering?

It's easy to see how lazy collections can be supported, since Hibernate can provide its own special implementations of the various Collection interfaces. But what about other kinds of associations? They might benefit from on–demand loading as well.

In fact, Hibernate does support this, and almost as easily (at least from our perspective as users of its services). The way you set this up is by marking an entire persistent class as `lazy="true"` (this attribute goes right in the `class` tag of the mapping document). When you do this, Hibernate will generate a proxy class that extends (and poses as) your data class. This lazy proxy puts off actually loading the data until it is needed. Any other objects with associations to the lazy class will sneakily be given these proxy objects, rather than references to your actual data object. The first time any of the methods of the proxy object are used, it will load the real data object and delegate the method call to it. Once the data object is loaded, the proxy simply continues delegating all method calls to it.

If you want to get fancier, you can specify a specific class (or interface) to be extended (or implemented) by the proxy class, using the `proxy` attribute. The `lazy` attribute is shorthand for specifying the persistent class itself as the type to be proxied. (If this is all incomprehensible, don't worry, that just means you don't yet need this capability. By the time you do, you'll understand it!)

Naturally, the same caveats about taking care to load anything you'll need to use before closing the session apply to this kind of lazy initialization too. If you need it, you can use it, but do so with care and planning.

The Hibernate reference documentation discusses these considerations in more depth in its chapter "Improving Performance." Also introduced there is the fact that Hibernate can be integrated with JVM-level or even clustered object caches to boost the performance of large, distributed applications, by reducing the bottleneck of database access. When plugged in to such a cache, the mapping document lets you configure the cache behavior of classes and associations using (appropriately enough) `cache` tags. These configurations go beyond what we cover in this notebook, but you should be aware that they're possible in case your application would benefit from them.

Ordered Collections

Oh, right, that's
what we were
going to try...

Our first goal is to store the tracks that make up an album, keeping them in the right order. Later we'll add information like the disc on which a track is found, and its position on that disc, so we can gracefully handle multi-disc albums.

How do I do that?

The task of keeping a collection in a particular order is actually straight-forward. If that's all we cared about in organizing album tracks, we'd need only tell Hibernate to map a List or array. In our Album mapping we'd use something like Example 5-2.

Example 5-2. Simple ordered mapping of tracks for an album

```
<list name="tracks" table="ALBUM_TRACKS">
  <key column="ALBUM_ID"/>
  <index column="POSITION"/>
  <many-to-many class="com.oreilly.hh.Track" column="TRACK_ID"/>
</list>
```

This is very much like the set mappings we've used so far (although it uses a different tag to indicate it's an ordered list and therefore maps to a java.util.List). But notice that we also need to add an index tag to establish the ordering of the list, and we need to add a column to hold the value controlling the ordering in the database. Hibernate will manage the contents of this column for us, and use it to ensure that when we get the list out of the database in the future, its contents will be in the same order in which we stored them. The column is created as an integer, and if possible, it is used as part of a composite key for the table. The mapping in Example 5-2, when used to generate a HSQLDB database schema, produces the table shown in Example 5-3.

Example 5-3. Our simple track list realized as an HSQLDB schema

```
[schemaexport] create table ALBUM_TRACKS (
[schemaexport]     ALBUM_ID INTEGER not null,
[schemaexport]     TRACK_ID INTEGER not null,
[schemaexport]     POSITION INTEGER not null,
[schemaexport]     primary key (ALBUM_ID, POSITION)
[schemaexport] )
```

It's important to understand why the POSITION column is necessary. We need to control the order in which tracks appear in an album, and there aren't any properties of the tracks themselves we can use to keep them sorted in the right order. (Imagine how annoyed you'd be if your jukebox system could only play the tracks of an album in, say, alphabetical order, regardless of the intent of the artists who created it!) The fundamental nature of relational database systems is that you get results in whatever order the system finds convenient, unless you tell it how to sort them. The POSITION column gives Hibernate a value under its control that can be used to ensure that our list is always sorted in the order in which we created it. Another way to think about this is that the order of the entries is one of the independent pieces of information we want to keep track of, so Hibernate needs a place to store it.

The corollary is also important. If there are values in your data that provide a natural order for traversal, there is no need for you to provide an index column; you don't even have to use a list. The set and map collection mappings can be configured to be sorted in Java by providing a sort attribute, or within the database itself by providing a SQL order-by attribute.* In either case, when you iterate over the contents of the collection, you'll get them in the specified order.

TIP

The values in the POSITION column will always be the same values you'd use as an argument to the tracks.get() method in order to obtain the value at a particular position in the tracks list.

Augmenting Associations in Collections

All right, we've got a handle on what we need to do if we want our albums' tracks to be kept in the right order. What about the additional information we'd like to keep, such as the disc on which the track is found? When we map a collection of associations, we've seen that Hibernate creates a join table in which to store the relationships between objects. And we've just seen how to add an index column to the ALBUM_ TRACKS table to maintain an ordering for the collection. Ideally, we'd like the ability to augment that table with more information of our own choosing, in order to record the other details we'd like to know about album tracks.

As it turns out, we can do just that, and in a very straightforward way.

How do I do that?

Up until this point we've seen two ways of getting tables into our database schema. The first was by explicitly mapping properties of a Java

---

* The order-by attribute and SQL sorting of collections is only available if you're using Version 1.4 or later of the Java SDK, since it relies on the LinkedHashSet or LinkedHashMap classes introduced in that release.

object onto columns of a table. The second was defining a collection of associations, and specifying the table and columns used to manage that collection. As it turns out, there's nothing that prevents us from using a single table in both ways. Some of its columns can be used directly to map to our own objects' properties, while the others can manage the mapping of a collection. This lets us achieve our goals of recording the tracks that make up an album in an ordered way, augmented by additional details to support multi-disc albums.

We'll want a new data object, AlbumTrack, to contain information about how a track is used on an album. Since we've already seen several examples of how to map full-blown entities with independent existence, and there really isn't a need for our AlbumTrack object to exist outside the context of an Album entity, this is a good opportunity to look at mapping a *component*. Recall that in Hibernate jargon an entity is an object that stands on its own in the persistence mechanism: it can be created, queried, and deleted independently of any other objects, and therefore has its own persistent identity (as reflected by its mandatory id property). A component, in contrast, is an object that can be saved to and retrieved from the database, but only as a subordinate part of some other entity. In this case, we'll define a list of AlbumTrack objects as a component part of our Album entity. Example 5-4 shows a mapping for the Album class that achieves this.

This flexibility took a little setting used to but it makes sense, especially if you think about mapping objects to an existing database schema.

Example 5-4. *Album.hbm.xml*, the mapping definition for an Album

```
1   <?xml version="1.0"?>
2   <!DOCTYPE hibernate-mapping PUBLIC "-//Hibernate/Hibernate Mapping DTD 2.0//EN"
3              "http://hibernate.sourceforge.net/hibernate-mapping-2.0.dtd">
4
5   <hibernate-mapping>
6     <class name="com.oreilly.hh.Album" table="ALBUM">
7       <meta attribute="class-description">
8         Represents an album in the music database, an organized list of tracks.
9         @author Jim Elliott (with help from Hibernate)
10      </meta>
11
12      <id name="id" type="int" column="ALBUM_ID">
13        <meta attribute="scope-set">protected</meta>
14        <generator class="native"/>
15      </id>
16
17      <property name="title" type="string">
18        <meta attribute="use-in-tostring">true</meta>
19        <column name="TITLE" not-null="true" index="ALBUM_TITLE"/>
20      </property>
21
22      <property name="numDiscs" type="integer"/>
23
```

Example 5-4. *Album.hbm.xml*, the mapping definition for an Album (continued)

```
24      <set name="artists" table="ALBUM_ARTISTS">
25        <key column="ALBUM_ID"/>
26        <many-to-many class="com.oreilly.hh.Artist" column="ARTIST_ID"/>
27      </set>
28
29      <set name="comments" table="ALBUM_COMMENTS">
30        <key column="ALBUM_ID"/>
31        <element column="COMMENT" type="string"/>
32      </set>
33
34      <list name="tracks" table="ALBUM_TRACKS">
35       <meta attribute="use-in-tostring">true</meta>
36        <key column="ALBUM_ID"/>
37        <index column="POSITION"/>
38        <composite-element class="com.oreilly.hh.AlbumTrack">
39          <many-to-one name="track" class="com.oreilly.hh.Track">
40            <meta attribute="use-in-tostring">true</meta>
41            <column name="TRACK_ID"/>
42          </many-to-one>
43          <property name="disc" type="integer"/>
44          <property name="positionOnDisc" type="integer"/>
45        </composite-element>
46      </list>
47
48      <property name="added" type="date">
49        <meta attribute="field-description">When the album was created</meta>
50      </property>
51
52    </class>
53  </hibernate-mapping>
```

A lot of this is similar to mappings we've seen before, but the tracks list (starting on line 34) is worth some careful examination. The discussion gets involved, so let's step back a minute and recall exactly what we're trying to accomplish.

We want our album to keep an ordered list of the tracks that make it up, along with additional information about each track that tells which disc it's on (in case the album has multiple discs) and the track's position within the disc. This conceptual relationship is shown in the middle of Figure 5-1. The association between albums and tracks is mediated by an "Album Tracks" object that adds disc and position information, as well as keeping them in the right order. The model of the tracks themselves is familiar (we're leaving out artist and comment information in this diagram, in an effort to keep it simpler). This model is what we've captured in the album mapping document, Example 5-4. Let's examine the details of how it was done. Later we'll look at how Hibernate turns this specification into Java code (the bottom part of Figure 5-1) and a database schema (the top part).

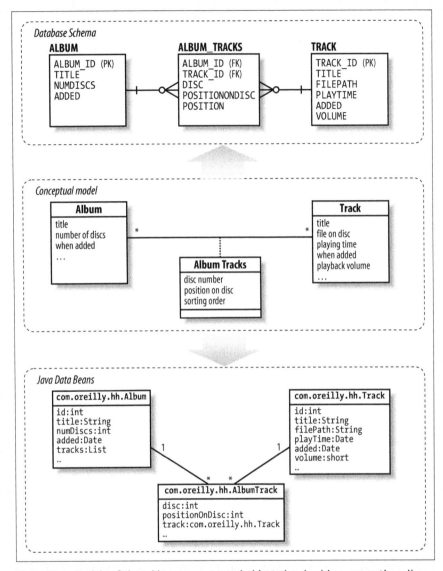

Figure 5-1. Models of the tables, concepts, and objects involved in representing album tracks

If you compare lines 34–46 of Example 5-4 with one of the set mappings in the preceding chapter, you'll see a lot of similarity. It looks even more like Example 5-2, except that the association mapping has been moved inside a new composite-element mapping, lines 38–45. This element introduces the new AlbumTrack object we use to group the disc, position, and Track link needed to organize an album's tracks. Also, rather than being a many-to-many mapping (because an album

---

generally has multiple tracks, and a given track file might be shared between several albums), the association between AlbumTrack and Track on line 39 is many-to-one: several AlbumTrack objects (from different albums) might refer to the same Track file if we're trying to save disk space, but each AlbumTrack object is concerned with only one Track. The list tag that contains AlbumTrack is implicitly one-to-many. (If you're still having trouble with these data modeling concepts, don't struggle too hard just now—the source code and schema coming up shortly will hopefully help you see what is happening here.)

Okay, back to this new composite-element definition. It specifies that we want to use a new AlbumTrack class as the values that appear in our Album data bean's tracks list. The body of the composite-element tag defines the properties of AlbumTrack, which group all the information we need about a track on an album. The syntax for these nested properties, lines 39–44, is no different than that of the outer mappings for Album's own properties. They can even include their own nested composite elements, collections, or (as seen here) meta attributes. This gives us tremendous flexibility to set up fine-grained mappings that retain a healthy degree of object-oriented encapsulation.

In our composite AlbumTrack mapping, we are recording an association with the actual Track (lines 39–42) to be played at each position within the Album, as well as the disc on which that track is found (line 43), and, on line 44, this entry's position on that disc (for example, track 3 of disc 2). This achieves the goals we started with and illustrates how arbitrary information can be attached to a collection of associations. The source for the class itself can be found in Example 5-5, and it might help clarify this discussion. Compare this source code with its graphical representation at the bottom of Figure 5-1.

You may have noticed that I chose an explicit column name of TRACK_ID to use for the many-to-one link to the TRACK table (line 41). I've actually been doing this in a number of places, but previously it didn't require an entire separate line. It's worth talking about the reasoning behind this choice. Without this instruction, Hibernate will just use the property name (track) for the column name. You can use any names you want for your columns, but *Java Database Best Practices* encourages naming foreign key columns the same as the primary keys in the original tables to which they refer. This helps data modeling tools recognize and display the "natural joins" the foreign keys represent, which makes it easier for people to understand and work with the data. This consideration is also why I included the table names as part of the primary keys' column names.

What just happened?

I was all set to explain that by choosing to use a composite element to encapsulate our augmented track list, we'd have to write the Java source for AlbumTrack ourselves. I was sure this went far beyond the capabilities of the code generation tool. Much to my delight, when I tried **ant codegen** to see what sort of errors would result, the command reported success, and both *Album.java* and *AlbumTrack.java* appeared in the source directory!

Sometimes it's nice to be proved wrong.

It was at this point that I went back and added the use-in-tostring meta attribute for the track many-to-one mapping inside the component. I wasn't sure this would work either, because the only examples of its use I've found in the reference manual are attached to actual property tags. But work it did, exactly as I hoped.

The Hibernate best practices encourage using fine-grained classes and mapping them as components. Given how easily the code generation tool allows you to create them from your mapping documents, there is absolutely no excuse for ignoring this advice. Example 5-5 shows the source generated for our nested composite mapping.

Example 5-5. Code generated for *AlbumTrack.java*

```java
package com.oreilly.hh;

import java.io.Serializable;
import org.apache.commons.lang.builder.ToStringBuilder;

/**
 *      Represents an album in the music database, an organized list of tracks.
 *      @author Jim Elliott (with help from Hibernate)
 *
 */
public class AlbumTrack implements Serializable {

    /** nullable persistent field */
    private int disc;

    /** nullable persistent field */
    private int positionOnDisc;

    /** nullable persistent field */
    private com.oreilly.hh.Track track;

    /** full constructor */
    public AlbumTrack(int disc, int positionOnDisc, com.oreilly.hh.Track track) {
        this.disc = disc;
        this.positionOnDisc = positionOnDisc;
```

Example 5-5. Code generated for *AlbumTrack.java (continued)*

```
        this.track = track;
    }

    /** default constructor */
    public AlbumTrack() {
    }

    public int getDisc() {
        return this.disc;
    }

    public void setDisc(int disc) {
        this.disc = disc;
    }

    public int getPositionOnDisc() {
        return this.positionOnDisc;
    }

    public void setPositionOnDisc(int positionOnDisc) {
        this.positionOnDisc = positionOnDisc;
    }

    public com.oreilly.hh.Track getTrack() {
        return this.track;
    }

    public void setTrack(com.oreilly.hh.Track track) {
        this.track = track;
    }

    public String toString() {
        return new ToStringBuilder(this)
            .append("track", getTrack())
            .toString();
    }

}
```

This looks similar to the generated code for entities we've seen in previous chapters, but it lacks an id property, which makes sense. Component classes don't need identifier fields, and they need not implement any special interfaces. The class JavaDoc is shared with the Album class, in which this component is used. The source of the Album class itself is a typical generated entity, so there's no need to reproduce it here.

At this point we can build the schema for these new mappings, via **ant schema**. Example 5-6 shows highlights of the resulting schema creation process. This is the concrete HSQLDB representation of the schema modeled at the top of Figure 5-1.

Example 5-6. Additions to the schema caused by our new Album mapping

```
[schemaexport] create table ALBUM (
[schemaexport]     ALBUM_ID INTEGER NOT NULL IDENTITY,
[schemaexport]     TITLE VARCHAR(255) not null,
[schemaexport]     numDiscs INTEGER,
[schemaexport]     added DATE
[schemaexport] )
...
[schemaexport] create table ALBUM_COMMENTS (
[schemaexport]     ALBUM_ID INTEGER not null,
[schemaexport]     COMMENT VARCHAR(255)
[schemaexport] )
...
[schemaexport] create table ALBUM_ARTISTS (
[schemaexport]     ALBUM_ID INTEGER not null,
[schemaexport]     ARTIST_ID INTEGER not null,
[schemaexport]     primary key (ALBUM, ARTIST)
[schemaexport] )
...
[schemaexport] create table ALBUM_TRACKS (
[schemaexport]     ALBUM_ID INTEGER not null,
[schemaexport]     TRACK_ID INTEGER,
[schemaexport]     disc INTEGER,
[schemaexport]     positionOnDisc INTEGER,
[schemaexport]     POSITION INTEGER not null,
[schemaexport]     primary key (ALBUM_ID, POSITION)
[schemaexport] )
...
[schemaexport] create index ALBUM_TITLE on ALBUM (title)
...
[schemaexport] alter table ALBUM_COMMENTS add constraint FK1E2C21E43B7864F
foreign key (ALBUM_ID) references ALBUM
...
[schemaexport] alter table ALBUM_ARTISTS add constraint FK7BA403FC3B7864F foreign
key (ALBUM_ID) references ALBUM
...
[schemaexport] alter table ALBUM_TRACKS add constraint FKD1CBBC783B7864F foreign
key (ALBUM_ID) references ALBUM
...
[schemaexport] alter table ALBUM_TRACKS add constraint FKD1CBBC78697F14B foreign
key (TRACK_ID) references TRACK
```

WARNING

You may find that making radical changes to the schema causes problems for Hibernate or the HSQLDB driver. When I switched between the above two approaches for mapping album tracks, I ran into trouble because the first set of mappings established database constraints that Hibernate didn't know to drop before trying to build the revised schema. This prevented it from dropping and recreating some tables. If this ever happens to you, you can delete the database file (*music.script* in the *data* directory) and start from scratch, which should work fine.

Figure 5-2 shows our enriched schema in HSQLDB's graphical management interface.

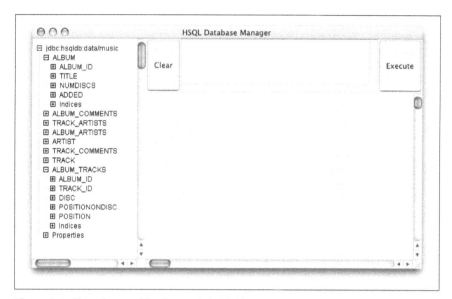

Figure 5-2. The schema with album-related tables

You might wonder why we use the separate Track class at all, rather than simply embedding all that information directly in our enhanced AlbumTracks collection. The simple answer is that not all tracks are part of an album—some might be singles, downloads, or otherwise independent. Given that we need a separate table to keep track of these anyway, it would be a poor design choice to duplicate its contents in the AlbumTracks table rather than associating with it. There is also a more subtle advantage to this approach, which is actually used in my own music database: this structure allows us to share a single track file between multiple albums. If the same song appears on an album, a "best of" collection, and one or more period collections or sound tracks, linking all these albums to the same track file saves disk space.

Let's look at some sample code showing how to use these new data objects. Example 5-7 shows a class that creates an album record and its list of tracks, then prints it out to test the debugging; support we've configured for the toString() method.

Example 5-7. Source of *AlbumTest.java*

```
1  package com.oreilly.hh;
2
3  import net.sf.hibernate.*;
```

Example 5-7. *Source of AlbumTest.java (continued)*

```
4   import net.sf.hibernate.cfg.Configuration;
5
6   import java.sql.Time;
7   import java.util.*;
8
9   /**
10   * Create sample album data, letting Hibernate persist it for us.
11   */
12  public class AlbumTest {
13
14      /**
15       * Quick and dirty helper method to handle repetitive portion of creating
16       * album tracks. A real implementation would have much more flexibility.
17       */
18      private static void addAlbumTrack(Album album, String title, String file,
19                                        Time length, Artist artist, int disc,
20                                        int positionOnDisc, Session session)
21          throws HibernateException
22      {
23          Track track = new Track(title, file, length, new Date(), (short)0,
24                                  new HashSet(), new HashSet());
25          track.getArtists().add(artist);
26          session.save(track);
27          album.getTracks().add(new AlbumTrack(disc, positionOnDisc, track));
28      }
29
30      public static void main(String args[]) throws Exception {
31          // Create a configuration based on the properties file we've put
32          // in the standard place.
33          Configuration config = new Configuration();
34
35          // Tell it about the classes we want mapped.
36          config.addClass(Track.class).addClass(Artist.class);
37          config.addClass(Album.class);
38
39          // Get the session factory we can use for persistence
40          SessionFactory sessionFactory = config.buildSessionFactory();
41
42          // Ask for a session using the JDBC information we've configured
43          Session session = sessionFactory.openSession();
44          Transaction tx = null;
45          try {
46              // Create some data and persist it
47              tx = session.beginTransaction();
48
49              Artist artist = CreateTest.getArtist("Martin L. Gore", true,
50                                                   session);
51              List albumTracks = new ArrayList(5);
52              Album album = new Album("Counterfeit e.p.", 1, new Date(),
53                                      albumTracks, new HashSet(), new HashSet());
54              album.getArtists().add(artist);
55              session.save(album);
56
```

Example 5-7. *Source of AlbumTest.java (continued)*

```
57              addAlbumTrack(album, "Compulsion", "vol1/album83/track01.mp3",
58                      Time.valueOf("00:05:29"), artist, 1, 1, session);
59              addAlbumTrack(album, "In a Manner of Speaking",
60                      "vol1/album83/track02.mp3", Time.valueOf("00:04:21"),
61                      artist, 1, 2, session);
62              addAlbumTrack(album, "Smile in the Crowd",
63                      "vol1/album83/track03.mp3", Time.valueOf("00:05:06"),
64                      artist, 1, 3, session);
65              addAlbumTrack(album, "Gone", "vol1/album83/track04.mp3",
66                      Time.valueOf("00:03:32"), artist, 1, 4, session);
67              addAlbumTrack(album, "Never Turn Your Back on Mother Earth",
68                      "vol1/album83/track05.mp3", Time.valueOf("00:03:07"),
69                      artist, 1, 5, session);
70              addAlbumTrack(album, "Motherless Child", "vol1/album83/track06.mp3",
71                      Time.valueOf("00:03:32"), artist, 1, 6, session);
72
73              System.out.println(album);
74
75              // We're done; make our changes permanent
76              tx.commit();
77
78          } catch (Exception e) {
79              if (tx != null) {
80                  // Something went wrong; discard all partial changes
81                  tx.rollback();
82              }
83              throw e;
84          } finally {
85              // No matter what, close the session
86              session.close();
87          }
88
89          // Clean up after ourselves
90          sessionFactory.close();
91      }
92  }
```

The addAlbumTrack() method starting on line 14 creates and persists a
Track object given the specified parameters, associates it with a single
Artist (line 25), then adds it to the supplied Album, recording the disc
it's on and its position within that disc (line 27). In this simple example
we're creating an album with just one disc. This quick-and-dirty method
can't cope with many variations, but it does allow the example to be
compressed nicely.

We also need a new target at the end of *build.xml* to invoke the class.
Add the lines of Example 5-8 at the end of the file (but inside the
project tag, of course).

Example 5-8. New target to run our album test class

```
<target name="atest" description="Creates and persists some album data"
        depends="compile">
  <java classname="com.oreilly.hh.AlbumTest" fork="true">
    <classpath refid="project.class.path"/>
  </java>
</target>
```

With this in place, assuming you've generated the schema, run **ant ctest** followed by **ant atest**. (Running ctest first is optional, but having some extra data in there to begin with makes the album data somewhat more interesting. Recall that you can run these targets in one command as **ant ctest atest**, and if you want to start by erasing the contents of the database first, you can invoke **ant schema ctest atest**.) The debugging output produced by this command is shown in Example 5-9. Although admittedly cryptic, you should be able to see that the album and tracks have been created, and the order of the tracks has been maintained.

Example 5-9. Output from running the album test

```
atest:
     [java] com.oreilly.hh.Album@863cc1[id=0,title=Counterfeit e.p.,tracks=[com.
oreilly.hh.AlbumTrack@b3cc96[track=com.oreilly.hh.
Track@fea539[id=7,title=Compulsion]], com.oreilly.hh.AlbumTrack@3ca972[track=com.
oreilly.hh.Track@f2e328[id=8,title=In a Manner of Speaking]], com.oreilly.hh.
AlbumTrack@98a1f4[track=com.oreilly.hh.Track@1f6c18[id=9,title=Smile in the
Crowd]], com.oreilly.hh.AlbumTrack@b0d990[track=com.oreilly.hh.
Track@f1cdfb[id=10,title=Gone]], com.oreilly.hh.AlbumTrack@9baf0b[track=com.
oreilly.hh.Track@a59d2[id=11,title=Never Turn Your Back on Mother Earth]], com.
oreilly.hh.AlbumTrack@10c69[track=com.oreilly.hh.
Track@8f1ed7[id=12,title=Motherless Child]]]]]
```

If we run our old query test, we can see both the old and new data, as in Example 5-10.

Example 5-10. All tracks are less than seven minutes long, whether from albums or otherwise

```
% ant qtest
Buildfile: build.xml
...
qtest:
     [java] Track: "Russian Trance" (PPK) 00:03:30
     [java] Track: "Video Killed the Radio Star" (The Buggles) 00:03:49
     [java] Track: "Gravity's Angel" (Laurie Anderson) 00:06:06
     [java] Track: "Adagio for Strings (Ferry Corsten Remix)" (Ferry Corsten,
William Orbit, Samuel Barber) 00:06:35
     [java] Track: "Test Tone 1" 00:00:10
     [java]    Comment: Pink noise to test equalization
     [java] Track: "Compulsion" (Martin L. Gore) 00:05:29
```

Example 5-10. All tracks are less than seven minutes long, whether from albums or otherwise (continued)

```
[java] Track: "In a Manner of Speaking" (Martin L. Gore) 00:04:21
[java] Track: "Smile in the Crowd" (Martin L. Gore) 00:05:06
[java] Track: "Gone" (Martin L. Gore) 00:03:32
[java] Track: "Never Turn Your Back on Mother Earth" (Martin L. Gore) 00:03:07
[java] Track: "Motherless Child" (Martin L. Gore) 00:03:32
```

```
BUILD SUCCESSFUL
Total time: 12 seconds
```

Finally, Figure 5-3 shows a query in the HSQLDB interface that examines the contents of the ALBUM_TRACKS table.

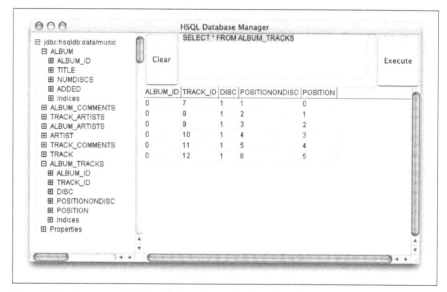

Figure 5-3. Our augmented collection of associations in action

Lifecycle Associations

Hibernate is completely responsible for managing the ALBUM_TRACKS table, adding and deleting rows (and, if necessary, renumbering POSITION values) as entries are added to or removed from Album beans' tracks properties. You can test this by writing a test program to delete the second track from our test album and see the result. A very quick and dirty way to do this would be to add the following four lines (see Example 5-11) right after the existing tx.commit() line in Example 5-7 and then run **ant schema ctest atest db**.

Example 5-11. Deleting our album's second track

```
tx = session.beginTransaction();
album.getTracks().remove(1);
session.update(album);
tx.commit();
```

Doing so changes the contents of ALBUM_TRACKS as shown in Figure 5-4 (compare this with the original contents in Figure 5-3). The second record has been removed (remember that Java list elements are indexed starting with zero), and POSITION has been adjusted so that it retains its consecutive nature, corresponding to the indices of the list elements (the values you'd use when calling tracks.get()).

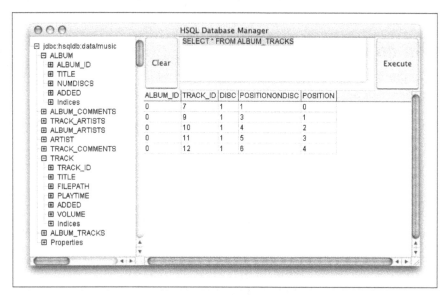

Figure 5-4. Album track associations after deleting our album's second track

This happens because Hibernate understands that this list is "owned" by the Album record, and that the "lifecycles" of the two objects are intimately connected. This notion of lifecycle becomes more clear if you consider what happens if the entire Album is deleted: all of the associated records in ALBUM_TRACKS will be deleted as well. (Go ahead and modify the test program to try this if you're not convinced.)

Contrast this with the relationship between the ALBUM table and the TRACK table. Tracks are sometimes associated with albums, but they are sometimes independent. Removing a track from the list got rid of a row in ALBUM_TRACKS, eliminating the link between the album and track, but didn't get rid of the row in TRACK, so it didn't delete the persistent Track object itself. Similarly, deleting the Album would eliminate all the associations in the collection, but none of the actual Tracks. It's the responsibility of our code to take care of that when appropriate (probably after consulting the user, in case any of the track records might be shared across multiple albums, as discussed above).

If we don't need the flexibility of sharing the same track between albums —disk space is pretty cheap lately given the size of compressed audio— we can let Hibernate manage the TRACK records for the album in the same way it does the ALBUM_TRACKS collection. It won't assume it should do this, because Track and Album objects can exist independently, but we can establish a lifecycle relationship between them in the album mapping document.

By now you're probably not surprised there's a way to automate this.

How do I do that?

Example 5-12 shows (in bold) the changes we'd make to the tracks property mapping in *Album.hbm.xml*.

Example 5-12. Establishing a lifecycle relationship between an album and its tracks

```
<list name="tracks" table="ALBUM_TRACKS" cascade="all">
  <meta attribute="use-in-tostring">true</meta>
  <key column="ALBUM_ID"/>
  <index column="POSITION"/>
  <composite-element class="com.oreilly.hh.AlbumTrack">
    <many-to-one name="track" class="com.oreilly.hh.Track" cascade="all">
      <meta attribute="use-in-tostring">true</meta>
      <column name="TRACK_ID"/>
    </many-to-one>
    <property name="disc" type="integer"/>
    <property name="positionOnDisc" type="integer"/>
  </composite-element>
</list>
```

The cascade attribute tells Hibernate that you want operations performed on a "parent" object to be transitively applied to its "child" or "dependent" objects. It's applicable to all forms of collections and associations. There are several possible values to choose among. The most common are none (the default), save-update, delete, and all (which combines save-update and delete). You can also change the default from none to save-update throughout your entire mapping document by supplying a default-cascade attribute in the hibernate-mapping tag itself.

In our example, we want the tracks owned by an album to be automatically managed by the album, so that when we delete the album, its tracks are deleted. Note that we need to apply the cascade attribute both to the `tracks` collection and its constituent `track` element to achieve this. Also, by using a `cascade` value of `all`, we eliminate the need to explicitly save any `Track` objects we create for the album—the `addAlbumTrack()` method of Example 5-7 no longer needs the line:

```
session.save(track);
```

By telling Hibernate that it's fully responsible for the relationship between an album and its track, we enable it to persist tracks when they're added to the album as well as delete them when the album itself is deleted.

Delegating this sort of bookkeeping to the mapping layer can be very convenient, freeing you to focus on more abstract and important tasks, so it is worth using when appropriate. It's reminiscent of the liberation provided by Java's pervasive garbage collection, but it can't be as comprehensive because there is no definitive way to know when you're finished with persistent data by performing reachability analysis; you need to indicate it by calling `delete()` and establishing lifecycle connections. The trade-off between flexibility and simple automation is yours to make, based on the nature of your data and the needs of your project.

WARNING

Hibernate's management of lifecycle relationships is not foolproof— or perhaps it's more accurate to say it's not all-encompassing. For example, if you use `Collections` methods to remove a `Track` from an `Album`'s `tracks` property, this breaks the link between the `Album` and `Track` but does *not* actually delete the `Track` record. Even if you later delete the entire `Album`, this `Track` will remain, because it wasn't linked to the `Album` at the time that it was deleted. Try some of these experiments by modifying *AlbumTest.java* appropriately and look at the resulting data in the tables!

Reflexive Associations

It's also possible for objects and tables to have associations back to themselves. This supports persistent recursive data structures like trees, in which nodes link to other nodes. Tracing through a database table storing such relationships using a SQL query interface is a major chore. Luckily, once it's mapped to Java objects, the process is much more readable and natural.

One way we might use a reflexive link in our music database is to allow alternate names for artists. This is useful more often than you might expect, because it makes it very easy to let the user find either "The Smiths" or "Smiths, The" depending on how they're thinking of the group, with little code, and in a language-independent way.

How do I do that?

All that's needed is to add another field to the Artist mapping in *Artist. hbm.xml*, establishing a link back to Artist. Example 5-13 shows one option.

Example 5-13. Supporting a reflexive association in the Artist class

```
<many-to-one name="actualArtist" class="com.oreilly.hh.Artist">
  <meta attribute="use-in-tostring">true</meta>
</many-to-one>
```

This gives us an actualArtist property that we can set to the id of the "definitive" Artist record when we're setting up an alternate name. For example, our "The Smiths" record might have id 5, and its actualArtist field would be null since it is definitive. Then we can create an "alias" Artist record with the name "Smiths, The" at any time, and set the actualArtist field in that record to point to record 5.

TIP

This kind of reflexive link is one instance where a column containing a foreign key can't be named the same as the key column to which it is a link. We are associating a row in ARTIST with another row in ARTIST, and of course the table already has a column named ARTIST_ID.

Why is this association set up as many-to-one? There might be many alias records that point to one particular definitive Artist. So each nickname needs to store the id of the actual artist record for which it is an alternative name. This is, in the language of data modeling, a many-to-one relationship.

Code that looks up artists just needs to check the actualArtist property before returning. If it's null, all is well. Otherwise it should return the record indicated by actualArtist. Example 5-14 shows how we could extend the getArtist() method in CreateTest to support this new feature (additions are in bold). Notice that the Artist constructor gets a new argument for setting actualArtist.

Example 5-14. *Artist lookup method supporting resolution of alternate names*

```
public static Artist getArtist(String name, boolean create,
                               Session session)
    throws HibernateException
{
    Query query = session.getNamedQuery(
                      "com.oreilly.hh.artistByName");
    query.setString("name", name);
    Artist found = (Artist)query.uniqueResult();
    if (found == null && create) {
        found = new Artist(name, null, new HashSet());
        session.save(found);
    }
    if (found != null && found.getActualArtist() != null) {
        return found.getActualArtist();
    }
    return found;
}
```

Hopefully this chapter has given you a feel for the rich and powerful ways you can use associations and collections in Hibernate. As should be obvious from the way you can nest and combine these capabilities, there are far more variations than we can hope to cover in a book like this.

The good news is that Hibernate seems well equipped to handle almost any kind of relationship your application might need, and it can even do the drudge work of building the data classes and database schema for you. This works much more effectively and deeply than I ever expected it would when I started creating these examples.

## CHAPTER 6

Persistent Enumerated Types

An *enumerated type* is a common and useful programming abstraction allowing a value to be selected from a fixed set of named choices. These were originally well represented in Pascal, but C took such a minimal approach (essentially just letting you assign symbolic names to interchangeable integer values) that early Java releases reserved C's enum keyword but declined to implement it. A better, object-oriented approach known as the "typesafe enum pattern" evolved and was popularized in Joshua Bloch's *Effective Java Programming Language Guide* (Addison-Wesley). This approach requires a fair amount of boilerplate coding, but it lets you do all kinds of interesting and powerful things. The Java 1.5 specification resuscitates the enum keyword as an easy way to get the power of typesafe enumerations without all the tedious boilerplate coding, and it provides other nifty benefits.

In this chapter:
* *Defining a Persistent Enumerated Type*
* *Working with Persistent Enumerations*

Regardless of how you implement an enumerated type, you're sometimes going to want to be able to persist such values to a database.

Defining a Persistent Enumerated Type

Hibernate has been around for a while and (at least as of this writing) Java 1.5 isn't yet released, so the support for enumerations in Hibernate can't take advantage of its new enum keyword. Instead, Hibernate lets you define your own typesafe enumeration classes however you like, and it provides a mechanism to help you get them into and out of a database, by translating them to and from small integer values. This is something of a regression to the world of C, but it is useful nonetheless.

C-style enumerations still appear too often in Java. Older parts of the Sun API contain many of them.

In our music database, for example, we might want to add a field to our Track class that tells us the medium from which it was imported.

How do I do that?

The key to adding persistence support for our enumeration is to have it implement Hibernate's PersistentEnum interface. This interface has two methods, toInt() and fromInt(), that Hibernate uses to translate between the enumeration constants and values that represent them in a database.

Let's suppose we want to be able to specify whether our tracks came from cassette tapes, vinyl, VHS tapes, CDs, a broadcast, an internet download site, or a digital audio stream. (We could go really nuts and distinguish between Internet streams and satellite radio services like Sirius or XM, or radio versus television broadcast, but this is plenty to demonstrate the important ideas.)

Without any consideration of persistence, our typesafe enumeration class might look something like Example 6-1. (The JavaDoc has been compressed to take less printed space, but the downloadable version is formatted normally.)

Example 6-1. *SourceMedia.java*, our initial typesafe enumeration

```
package com.oreilly.hh;

import java.util.*;
import java.io.Serializable;

/**
 * This is a typesafe enumeration that identifies the media on which an
 * item in our music database was obtained.
 **/
public class SourceMedia implements Serializable {

    /** Stores the external name of this instance, by which it can be retrieved. */
    private final String name;

    /**
     * Stores the human-readable description of this instance, by which it is
     * identified in the user interface.
     */
```

```
    private final transient String description;

    /**
     * Return the external name associated with this instance.
     * @return the name by which this instance is identified in code.
     **/
    public String getName() {
        return name;
    }

    /**
     * Return the description associated with this instance.
     * @return the human-readable description by which this instance is
     *         identified in the user interface.
     **/
    public String getDescription() {
        return description;
    }

    /** Keeps track of all instances by name, for efficient lookup. */
    private static final Map instancesByName = new HashMap();

    /**
     * Constructor is private to prevent instantiation except during class
     * loading.
     *
     * @param name the external name of the message type.
     * @param description the human readable description of the message type,
     *         by which it is presented in the user interface.
     */
    private SourceMedia(String name, String description) {
        this.name = name;
        this.description = description;

        // Record this instance in the collection that tracks the enumeration
        instancesByName.put(name, this);
    }

    /** The instance that represents music obtained from cassette tape. */
    public static final SourceMedia CASSETTE =
        new SourceMedia("cassette", "Audio Cassette Tape");

    /** The instance that represents music obtained from vinyl. */
    public static final SourceMedia VINYL =
        new SourceMedia("vinyl", "Vinyl Record");

    /** The instance that represents music obtained from VHS tapes. */
    public static final SourceMedia VHS =
        new SourceMedia("vhs", "VHS Videocassette Tape");

    /** The instance that represents music obtained from a compact disc. */
    public static final SourceMedia CD =
```

```
        new SourceMedia("cd", "Compact Disc");

    /** The instance that represents music obtained from a broadcast. */
    public static final SourceMedia BROADCAST =
        new SourceMedia("broadcast", "Analog Broadcast");

    /** The instance that represents music obtained as an Internet download. */
    public static final SourceMedia DOWNLOAD =
        new SourceMedia("download", "Internet Download");

    /** The instance that represents music from a digital audio stream. */
    public static final SourceMedia STREAM =
        new SourceMedia("stream", "Digital Audio Stream");

    /**
     * Obtain the collection of all legal enumeration values.
     * @return all instances of this typesafe enumeration.
     */
    public static Collection getAllValues() {
        return Collections.unmodifiableCollection(instancesByName.values());
    }

    /**
     * Look up an instance by name.
     *
     * @param name the external name of an instance.
     * @return the corresponding instance.
     * @throws NoSuchElementException if there is no such instance.
     */
    public static SourceMedia getInstanceByName(String name) {
        SourceMedia result = (SourceMedia)instancesByName.get(name);
        if (result == null) {
            throw new NoSuchElementException(name);
        }
        return result;
    }

    /** Return a string representation of this object. */
    public String toString() {
    return description;
    }

    /** Insure that deserialization preserves the signleton property. */
    private Object readResolve() {
        return getInstanceByName(name);
    }
}
```

To add persistence support for this class, all we need to do is implement the PersistentEnum interface. Unfortunately, this requires us to assign an integer value to each instance, and to provide a way of looking up

---

instances by this integer value. This is the "regression to C" mentioned in the introduction. Most typesafe enumerations with which I've worked have not included such an integer representation, since (as in this example) it was not part of their object-oriented semantics. Still, adding this integer property is not that hard. Example 6-2 shows the revisions we need to make in bold. (To save space, unchanged members and methods and some JavaDoc are omitted from this version of the example; the downloadable version is complete.)

Example 6-2. Changes to *SourceMedia.java* in order to support persistence using Hibernate

```
package com.oreilly.hh;

import net.sf.hibernate.PersistentEnum;
import java.util.*;
import java.io.Serializable;

/**
 * This is a typesafe enumeration that identifies the media on which an
 * item in our music database was obtained.
 **/
public class SourceMedia implements PersistentEnum, Serializable {
    ...
    /** Stores the integer value used by Hibernate to persist this instance. */
    private final int code;
    ...
    /**
     * Return the persistence code associated with this instance, as
     * mandated by the {@link PersistentEnum} interface.
     */
    public int toInt() {
        return code;
    }
    ...
    /** Keeps track of all instances by code, for efficient lookup. */
    private static final Map instancesByCode = new HashMap();

    /**
     * Constructor is private to prevent instantiation except during class
     * loading.
     *
     * @param name the external name of the message type.
     * @param description the human readable description of the message type,
     *        by which it is presented in the user interface.
     * @param code the persistence code by which Hibernate stores the instance.
     */
    private SourceMedia(String name, String description, int code) {
        this.name = name;
        this.description = description;
        this.code = code;
```

```
        // Record this instance in the collections that track the enumeration
        instancesByName.put(name, this);
        instancesByCode.put(new Integer(code), this);
    }
    ...
    public static final SourceMedia CASSETTE =
        new SourceMedia("cassette", "Audio Cassette Tape", 0);
    ...
    public static final SourceMedia VINYL =
        new SourceMedia("vinyl", "Vinyl Record", 1);
    ...
    public static final SourceMedia VHS =
        new SourceMedia("vhs", "VHS Videocassette Tape", 2);
    ...
    public static final SourceMedia CD =
        new SourceMedia("cd", "Compact Disc", 3);
    ...
    public static final SourceMedia BROADCAST =
        new SourceMedia("broadcast", "Analog Broadcast", 4);
    ...
    public static final SourceMedia DOWNLOAD =
        new SourceMedia("download", "Internet Download", 5);
    ...
    public static final SourceMedia STREAM =
        new SourceMedia("stream", "Digital Audio Stream", 6);
    ...
    /**
     * Look up an instance by code, as specified by the {@link PersistentEnum}
     * interface.
     *
     * @param code the persistence code of an instance.
     * @return the corresponding instance.
     * @throws NoSuchElementException if there is no such instance.
     */
    public static SourceMedia fromInt(int code) {
        SourceMedia result =
            (SourceMedia)instancesByCode.get(new Integer(code));
        if (result == null) {
            throw new NoSuchElementException("code=" + code);
        }
        return result;
    }
    ...
}
```

An alternative to adding the codes to the constructor arguments is to use a static counter that gets incremented each time a new instance is constructed. Although this is more convenient and concise, it makes it much harder to tell by inspection which code goes with which instance, and it also means you need to be careful to add any new instances to the end of the construction code if you don't want existing values to be rearranged (this is a problem if you've already got values persisted in the database). These are some of the reasons it'd be nicer to avoid the numeric codes completely, and use the symbolic names to represent instances in the database.

If you're in too much suspense, rest assured that the next chapter shows a nice way to avoid the need for such numeric codes.

The good news is that once we've got our persistent enum type defined, it's extremely easy to use it. Let's see how!

Working with Persistent Enumerations

If you were thinking about it, you may have noticed that we never defined a persistence mapping for the SourceMedia class in the first part of this chapter. That's because our persistent enumerated type is a *value* that gets persisted as part of one or more entities, rather than being an entity unto itself.

In that light, it's not surprising that we've not yet done any mapping. That happens when it's time to actually use the persistent enumeration.

How do I do that?

Recall that we wanted to keep track of the source media for the music tracks in our jukebox system. That means we want to use the SourceMedia enumeration in our Track mapping. We can simply add a new property tag to the class definition in *Track.hbm.xml*, as shown in Example 6-3.

Example 6-3. Adding the sourceMedia property to the Track mapping document

```
...
<property name="volume" type="short">
  <meta attribute="field-description">How loud to play the track</meta>
</property>

<property name="sourceMedia" type="com.oreilly.hh.SourceMedia">
  <meta attribute="field-description">Media on which track was obtained</meta>
  <meta attribute="use-in-tostring">true</meta>
</property>
```

Example 6-3. *Adding the sourceMedia property to the Track mapping document*

```
</class>
...
```

Because the type of our sourceMedia property names a class that implements the PersistentEnum interface, Hibernate knows to persist it using its built-in enumeration support.

With this addition in place, running **ant codegen** updates our Track class to include the new property. The signature of the full-blown Track constructor now looks like this:

```
public Track(String title, String filePath, Date playTime, Date added,
        short volume, com.oreilly.hh.SourceMedia sourceMedia,
        Set artists, Set comments) { ... }
```

We need to make corresponding changes in *CreateTest.java*:

```
Track track = new Track("Russian Trance",
                "vol2/album610/track02.mp3",
                Time.valueOf("00:03:30"), new Date(),
                (short)0, SourceMedia.CD,
                new HashSet(), new HashSet());
    ...
        track = new Track("Video Killed the Radio Star",
                "vol2/album611/track12.mp3",
                Time.valueOf("00:03:49"), new Date(),
                (short)0, SourceMedia.VHS,
                new HashSet(), new HashSet());
```

And so on. To match the results shown later, mark the rest as coming from CDs, except for "The World '99" which comes from a stream and give "Test Tone 1" a null sourceMedia value. At this point, run **ant schema** to rebuild the database schema with support for the new property, and run **ant ctest** to create the sample data.

What just happened?

Our TRACK table now contains an integer column to store the sourceMedia property. We can see its values by looking at the contents of the table after creating the sample data (the easiest way is to run a query within **ant db**, as shown in Figure 6-1).

We can verify that the values persisted to the database are correct by cross-checking the codes assigned to our persistent enumeration. Alternately, we can see a more meaningful version of the information by slightly enhancing the query test to print this property for the tracks it retrieves. The necessary changes are in bold in Example 6-4.

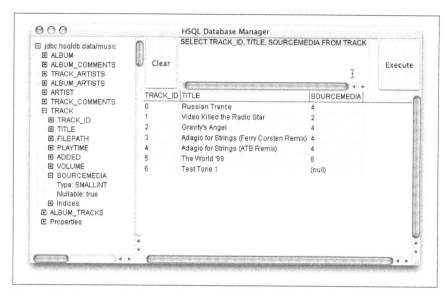

Figure 6-1. Source media information in the TRACK table

Example 6-4. Displaying source media in *QueryTest.java*

```
...
// Print the tracks that will fit in seven minutes
List tracks = tracksNoLongerThan(Time.valueOf("00:07:00"),
                                 session);
for (ListIterator iter = tracks.listIterator() ;
    iter.hasNext() ; ) {
    Track aTrack = (Track)iter.next();
    String mediaInfo = "";
    if (aTrack.getSourceMedia() != null) {
        mediaInfo = ", from " +
            aTrack.getSourceMedia().getDescription();
    }
    System.out.println("Track: \"" + aTrack.getTitle() + "\" " +
                    listArtistNames(aTrack.getArtists()) +
                    aTrack.getPlayTime() + mediaInfo);
```

With these enhancements, running **ant qtest** yields the output shown in
Example 6-5. Tracks with non-null source media values now have
"from" and the appropriate media description displayed at the end.

Example 6-5. Human-oriented display of source media information

```
...
qtest:
     [java] Track: "Russian Trance" (PPK) 00:03:30, from Compact Disc
     [java] Track: "Video Killed the Radio Star" (The Buggles) 00:03:49, from VHS
Videocassette Tape
     [java] Track: "Gravity's Angel" (Laurie Anderson) 00:06:06, from Compact Disc
```

Example 6-5. Human-oriented display of source media information (continued)

```
    [java] Track: "Adagio for Strings (Ferry Corsten Remix)" (Ferry Corsten,
William Orbit, Samuel Barber) 00:06:35, from Compact Disc
    [java] Track: "Test Tone 1" 00:00:10
    [java]   Comment: Pink noise to test equalization
```

Note that if we hadn't decided to do our own fancy formatting of a subset of the tracks' properties in QueryTest and instead relied on the toString() method in Track, we'd not have needed to make any changes to QueryTest to see this new information. Our mapping document specified that the sourceMedia property should be included in the toString() result, which would have taken care of it. You can inspect the generated toString() source to check this, or write a simple test program to see what the toString() output looks like. An excellent candidate would be to fix AlbumTest.java so it will compile and run after our changes to Track. The easiest fix is to simply hardcode the addAlbumTrack() method to assume everything comes from CDs, as in Example 6-5 (the JavaDoc already excuses such shameful rigidity).

Example 6-6. Fixing *AlbumTest.java* to support source media

```
/**
 * Quick and dirty helper method to handle repetitive portion of creating
 * album tracks. A real implementation would have much more flexibility.
 */
private static void addAlbumTrack(Album album, String title, String file,
                                  Time length, Artist artist, int disc,
                                  int positionOnDisc, Session session)
        throws HibernateException
{
    Track track = new Track(title, file, length, new Date(), (short)0,
                    SourceMedia.CD, new HashSet(), new HashSet());
    track.getArtists().add(artist);
    //       session.save(track);
    album.getTracks().add(new AlbumTrack(disc, positionOnDisc, track));
}
```

With this fix in place, running **ant atest** shows that the source media information propagates all the way up to Album's own toString() method:

```
    [java] com.oreilly.hh.Album@e0f945[id=0,title=Counterfeit e.p.,
tracks=[com.oreilly.hh.AlbumTrack@1370ab[track=com.oreilly.hh.
Track@49f9fa[id=<null>,title=Compulsion,sourceMedia=Compact Disc]], com.
oreilly.hh.AlbumTrack@ba936a[track=com.oreilly.hh.Track@2421db[id=<null>,
title=In a Manner of Speaking,sourceMedia=Compact Disc]], com.oreilly.hh.
AlbumTrack@2ad974[track=com.oreilly.hh.Track@2a7640[id=<null>,title=Smile in
the Crowd,sourceMedia=Compact Disc]], com.oreilly.hh.
AlbumTrack@b9808e[track=com.oreilly.hh.Track@a721e2[id=<null>,
```

```
title=Gone,sourceMedia=Compact Disc]], com.oreilly.hh.
AlbumTrack@a1ad7d[track=com.oreilly.hh.Track@851576[id=<null>,title=Never
Turn Your Back on Mother Earth,sourceMedia=Compact Disc]], com.oreilly.hh.
AlbumTrack@442c19[track=com.oreilly.hh.Track@ab2ddb[id=<null>,
title=Motherless Child,sourceMedia=Compact Disc]]]]
```

With a little work, Hibernate lets you extend your typesafe enumerations to support persistence. And once you've invested that effort, you can persist them as easily as any other value type for which native support exists.

It will be interesting to see how Hibernate evolves to take advantage of the exciting enum keyword support in Java 1.5 once that's been out for a while. The need to implement PersistentEnum will probably disappear, since all real enums will already extend java.lang.Enum and will have interesting ways to obtain specific members. I hope that as Hibernate evolves to support these new first-class enumerations, it will also allow their symbolic enumeration constants to be stored in the database, rather than requiring the use of a cryptic integer column as it does today. In an ideal world, it will even be able to take advantage of the native support for enumerations provided by some databases.

If you're interested in an alternate approach to persisting typesafe enumerations that can achieve some of these goals today, read on to Chapter 7 in which the mysteries of custom type mapping are explored!

Custom Value Types

Hibernate supports a wealth of Java types, be they simple values or objects, as you can see by skimming Appendix A. By setting up mapping specifications, you can persist even highly complex, nested object structures to arbitrary database tables and columns. With all this power and flexibility, you might wonder why you'd ever need to go beyond the built-in type support.

One situation that might motivate you to customize Hibernate's type support is if you want to use a different SQL column type to store a particular Java type than Hibernate normally chooses. The reference documentation cites the example of persisting Java BigInteger values into VARCHAR columns, which might be necessary to accommodate a legacy database schema.

Another scenario that requires the ability to tweak the type system is when you have a single property value that needs to get split into more than one database column—maybe the Address object in your company's mandated reuse library stores ZIP+4 codes as a single string, but the database to which you're integrating contains a required five digit column and a separate nullable four digit column for the two components. Or maybe it's the other way around, and you need to separate a single database column into more than one property.

Luckily, in situations like this, Hibernate lets you take over the details of the persistence mapping so you can fit square pegs into round holes when you really need to.

You might also want to build a custom value type even in some cases where it's not strictly necessary. If you've got a composite type that is

In this chapter:
- *Defining a User Type*
- *Using a Custom Type Mapping*
- *Building a Composite User Type*

Continuing in the spirit of making simple things easy and complex things possible...

used in many places throughout your application (a vector, complex number, address, or the like), you can certainly map each of these occurrences as components, but it might be worth encapsulating the details of the mapping in a shared, reusable Java class rather than propagating the details throughout each of the mapping documents. That way, if the details of the mapping ever need to change for any reason, you've only got one class to fix rather than many individual component mappings to hunt down and adjust.

Defining a User Type

In all of these scenarios, the task is to teach Hibernate a new way to translate between a particular kind of in-memory value and its persistent database representation.

Hibernate lets you provide your own logic for mapping values in situations that need it, by implementing one of two interfaces: `net.sf.hibernate.UserType` or `net.sf.hibernate.CompositeUserType`.

It's important to realize that what is being created is a *translator* for a particular kind of value, not a new kind of value that knows how to persist itself. In other words, in our ZIP code example, it's not the ZIP code property that would implement `UserType`. Instead, we'd create a new class implementing `UserType`, and in our mapping document specify this class as the Java type used to map the ZIP code property. Because of this, I think the terminology of "user types" is a little confusing.

Let's look at a concrete example. In Chapter 6 we saw how to use Hibernate's built-in enumeration support to persist a typesafe enumeration to an integer column, and we had to work around the fact that many object-oriented enumerations have no natural integer representation. While we can hope that Java 1.5 will allow Hibernate to resolve this tension in a universal way, we don't have to wait for that to happen, nor do we necessarily have to make the kind of compromises we did in Example 6-2. We can define our own custom value type that persists the `SourceMedia` class on its own terms. Later in the chapter we'll look at a more complex example involving multiple properties and columns.

How do I do that?

We'll work with the verson of *SourceMedia.java* shown in Example 6-1. Our custom type will allow this class to be persisted without any changes from its original form. In other words, the design of our data classes can be dictated by the needs and semantics of the application alone, and we can move the persistence support into a separate class focused on that sole purpose. This is a much better division of labor.

We'll call our new class SourceMediaType. Our next decision is whether it needs to implement UserType or CompositeUserType. The reference documentation doesn't provide much guidance on this question, but the API documentation confirms the hint contained in the interface names: the CompositeUserType interface is only needed if your custom type implementation is to expose internal structure in the form of named properties that can be accessed individually in queries (as in our ZIP code example). For SourceMedia, a simple UserType implementation is sufficient. The source for a mapping manager meeting our needs is shown in Example 7-1.

Example 7-1. *SourceMediaType.java*, our custom type mapping handler

```
package com.oreilly.hh;

import java.io.Serializable;
import java.sql.PreparedStatement;
import java.sql.ResultSet;
import java.sql.SQLException;
import java.sql.Types;

import net.sf.hibernate.UserType;
import net.sf.hibernate.Hibernate;
import net.sf.hibernate.HibernateException;
import net.sf.hibernate.type.Type;

/**
 * Manages persistence for the {@link SourceMedia} typesafe enumeration.
 */
public class SourceMediaType implements UserType {

    /**
     * Indicates whether objects managed by this type are mutable.
     *
     * @return <code>false</code>, since enumeration instances are immutable
     *          singletons.
     */
    public boolean isMutable() {
        return false;
    }

    /**
     * Return a deep copy of the persistent state, stopping at
     * entities and collections.
     *
     * @param value the object whose state is to be copied.
     * @return the same object, since enumeration instances are singletons.
     * @throws ClassCastException for non {@link SourceMedia} values.
     */
```

Example 7-1. *SourceMediaType.java*, our custom type mapping handler (continued)

```java
public Object deepCopy(Object value) {
    return (SourceMedia)value;
}

/**
 * Compare two instances of the class mapped by this type for persistence
 * "equality".
 *
 * @param x first object to be compared.
 * @param y second object to be compared.
 * @return <code>true</code> iff both represent the same SourceMedia type.
 * @throws ClassCastException if x or y isn't a {@link SourceMedia}.
 */
public boolean equals(Object x, Object y) {
    // We can compare instances, since SourceMedia are immutable singletons
    return (x == y);
}

/**
 * Determine the class that is returned by {@link #nullSafeGet}.
 *
 * @return {@link SourceMedia}, the actual type returned
 * by {@link #nullSafeGet}.
 */
public Class returnedClass() {
    return SourceMedia.class;
}

/**
 * Determine the SQL type(s) of the column(s) used by this type mapping.
 *
 * @return a single VARCHAR column.
 */
public int[] sqlTypes() {
    // Allocate a new array each time to protect against callers changing
    // its contents.
    int[] typeList = {
        Types.VARCHAR
    };
    return typeList;
}

/**
 * Retrieve an instance of the mapped class from a JDBC {@link ResultSet}.
 *
 * @param rs the results from which the instance should be retrieved.
 * @param names the columns from which the instance should be retrieved.
 * @param owner the entity containing the value being retrieved.
 * @return the retrieved {@link SourceMedia} value, or <code>null</code>.
 * @throws HibernateException if there is a problem performing the mapping.
 * @throws SQLException if there is a problem accessing the database.
 */
```

Example 7-1. *SourceMediaType.java, our custom type mapping handler (continued)*

```java
public Object nullSafeGet(ResultSet rs, String[] names, Object owner)
    throws HibernateException, SQLException
{
    // Start by looking up the value name
    String name = (String) Hibernate.STRING.nullSafeGet(rs, names[0]);
    if (name == null) {
        return null;
    }
    // Then find the corresponding enumeration value
    try {
        return SourceMedia.getInstanceByName(name);
    }
    catch (java.util.NoSuchElementException e) {
        throw new HibernateException("Bad SourceMedia value: " + name, e);
    }
}


/**
 * Write an instance of the mapped class to a {@link PreparedStatement},
 * handling null values.
 *
 * @param st a JDBC prepared statement.
 * @param value the SourceMedia value to write.
 * @param index the parameter index within the prepared statement at which
 *          this value is to be written.
 * @throws HibernateException if there is a problem performing the mapping.
 * @throws SQLException if there is a problem accessing the database.
 */
public void nullSafeSet(PreparedStatement st, Object value, int index)
    throws HibernateException, SQLException
{
    String name = null;
    if (value != null)
        name = ((SourceMedia)value).getName();
    Hibernate.STRING.nullSafeSet(st, name, index);
}
}
```

All of the methods in this class are required by the UserType interface. Our implementations are quite brief and straightforward, as befits the simple mapping we've undertaken. The first three methods don't need any discussion beyond what's in the JavaDoc and inline comments.

The sqlTypes() method reports to Hibernate the number of columns that will be needed to store values managed by this custom type and the SQL types. We indicate that our type uses a single VARCHAR column.

In `nullSafeGet()` we translate database results into the corresponding `MediaSource` enumeration value. Since we know we stored the value as a string in the database, we can delegate the actual retrieval to Hibernate's utility method for loading strings from database results. You'll be able to do something like this in most cases. Then it's just a matter of using the enumeration's own instance lookup capability.

Mapping the other direction is handled by `nullSafeSet()`. Once again we can rely on built-in features of the enumeration to translate from a `MediaSource` instance to its name, and then use Hibernate's utilities to store this string in the database.

Using a Custom Type Mapping

All right, we've created a custom type persistence handler, and it wasn't so bad! Now it's time to actually use it to persist our enumeration data the way we want it.

How do I do that?

This is actually almost embarrassingly easy. Once we've got the value class, `SourceMedia`, and the persistence manager, `SourceMediaType`, in place, all we need to do is modify any mapping documents that were previously referring to the raw value type to refer instead to the custom persistence manager.

In our case, that means we change the mapping for the `mediaSource` property in *Track.hbm.xml* so it looks like Example 7-2 rather than Example 6-3.

That's it. No, really!

Example 7-2. Custom type mapping for the sourceMedia property

```
<property name="sourceMedia" type="com.oreilly.hh.SourceMediaType">
  <meta attribute="field-description">Media on which track was obtained</meta>
  <meta attribute="use-in-tostring">true</meta>
</property>
```

At this point, running **ant schema** will rebuild the database schema, changing the SOURCEMEDIA column in the TRACK table from integer to VARCHAR (as specified by SourceMediaType's sqlTypes() method).

Thanks to the beauty of letting the object/relational mapping layer handle the details of how data is stored and retrieved, we don't need to change any aspect of the example or test code that we were using in Chapter 6. You can run **ant ctest** to create sample data. It will run with no complaint. If you fire up **ant db** to look at the way it's stored, you'll find that our goal of storing semantically meaningful enumeration symbols has been achieved, as shown in Figure 7-1.

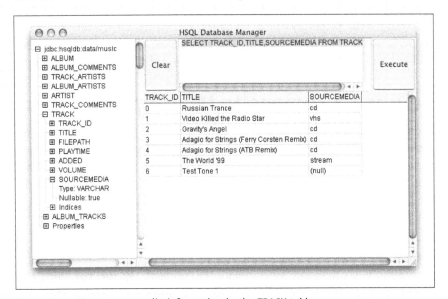

Figure 7-1. Nicer source media information in the TRACK table

Getting the data back out works just as well. Running **ant qtest** produces output that is identical to what we obtained when we were using

Hibernate's built-in, numeric enumeration support. Try it yourself, or compare Example 7-3 with Example 6-5.

Example 7-3. You can't tell the difference at the application layer

```
...
qtest:
    [java] Track: "Russian Trance" (PPK) 00:03:30, from Compact Disc
    [java] Track: "Video Killed the Radio Star" (The Buggles) 00:03:49, from VHS
Videocassette Tape
    [java] Track: "Gravity's Angel" (Laurie Anderson) 00:06:06, from Compact Disc
    [java] Track: "Adagio for Strings (Ferry Corsten Remix)" (Ferry Corsten,
William Orbit, Samuel Barber) 00:06:35, from Compact Disc
    [java] Track: "Test Tone 1" 00:00:10
    [java]    Comment: Pink noise to test equalization
...
```

Encapsulation and abstraction are wonderful things, aren't they?

What about...

...More complicated custom type mappings, such as splitting single properties into multiple database columns, or single columns into multiple properties? As noted earlier, your persistence handler class needs to implement CompositeUserType instead of UserType to provide this service. That interface adds only a few more methods for you to flesh out, and they deal primarily with teaching Hibernate about the synthetic properties you want to make available in queries, and providing ways for it to get and set the values of these properties. Let's look at an example!

Building a Composite User Type

Recall that in our Track object we have a property that determines our preferred playback volume for the track. Suppose we'd like the jukebox system to be able to adjust the *balance* of tracks for playback, rather than just their volume. To accomplish this we'd need to store separate volumes for the left and right channels. The quick solution would be to edit the Track mapping to store these as separate mapped properties.

If we're serious about object-oriented architecture, we might want to encapsulate these two values into a StereoVolume class. This class could then simply be mapped as a composite-element, as we did with the AlbumTrack component in lines 38–45 of Example 5-4. This is still fairly straightforward.

There is a drawback to this simple approach. It's likely we will discover other places in our system where we want to represent StereoVolume values. If we build a playlist mechanism that can override a track's default playback options, and also want to be able to assign volume control to entire albums, suddenly we have to recreate the composite mapping in several places, and we might not do it consistently everywhere (this is more likely to be an issue with a more complex compound type, but you get the idea). The Hibernate reference documentation says that it's a good practice to use a composite user type in situations like this, and I agree.

How do I do that?

Let's start by defining the StereoVolume class. There's no reason for this to be an entity (to have its own existence independent of some other persistent object), so we'll write it as an ordinary (and rather simple) Java object. Example 7-4 shows the source.

The JavaDoc in this example has been compressed to take less space. I'm trusting you not to do this in real projects... the downloadable version is more complete.

Example 7-4. *StereoVolume.java,* which is a value class representing a stereo volume level

```
1  package com.oreilly.hh;
2
3  import java.io.Serializable;
4
5  /**
6   * A simple structure encapsulating a stereo volume level.
7   */
8  public class StereoVolume implements Serializable {
9
10     /** The minimum legal volume level. */
11     public static final short MINIMUM = 0;
12
13     /** The maximum legal volume level. */
14     public static final short MAXIMUM = 100;
15
16     /** Stores the volume of the left channel. */
17     private short left;
18
19     /** Stores the volume of the right channel. */
20     private short right;
21
22     /** Default constructor sets full volume in both channels. */
23     public StereoVolume() {
24         this(MAXIMUM, MAXIMUM);
25     }
26
27     /** Constructor that establishes specific volume levels. */
28     public StereoVolume(short left, short right) {
29         setLeft(left);
30         setRight(right);
31     }
32
```

```
33      /**
34       * Helper method to make sure a volume value is legal.
35       * @param volume the level that is being set.
36       * @throws IllegalArgumentException if it is out of range.
37       */
38      private void checkVolume(short volume) {
39          if (volume < MINIMUM) {
40              throw new IllegalArgumentException("volume cannot be less than " +
41                                                  MINIMUM);
42          }
43          if (volume > MAXIMUM) {
44              throw new IllegalArgumentException("volume cannot be more than " +
45                                                  MAXIMUM);
46          }
47      }
48
49      /** Set the volume of the left channel. */
50      public void setLeft(short volume) {
51          checkVolume(volume);
52          left = volume;
53      }
54
55      /** Set the volume of the right channel. */
56      public void setRight(short volume) {
57          checkVolume(volume);
58          right = volume;
59      }
60
61      /** Get the volume of the left channel */
62      public short getLeft() {
63          return left;
64      }
65
66      /** Get the volume of the right channel. */
67      public short getRight() {
68          return right;
69      }
70
71      /** Format a readable version of the volume levels. */
72      public String toString() {
73          return "Volume[left=" + left + ", right=" + right + ']';
74      }
75
76      /**
77       * Compare whether another object is equal to this one.
78       * @param obj the object to be compared.
79       * @return true if obj is also a StereoVolume instance, and represents
80       *         the same volume levels.
81       */
82      public boolean equals(Object obj) {
83          if (obj instanceof StereoVolume) {
```

```
84                StereoVolume other = (StereoVolume)obj;
85                return other.getLeft() == getLeft() &&
86                    other.getRight() == getRight();
87            }
88            return false;  // It wasn't a StereoVolume
89        }
90
91        /**
92         * Returns a hash code value for the StereoVolume. This method must be
93         * consistent with the {@link #equals} method.
94         */
95        public int hashCode() {
96            return (int)getLeft() * MAXIMUM * 10 + getRight();
97        }
98    }
```

Since we want to be able to persist this with Hibernate, we provide a default constructor (lines 22–25) and property accessors (lines 49–69). Correct support for the Java equals() and hashCode() contracts is also important, since this is a mutable value object (lines 76 to the end).

To let us persist this as a composite type, rather than defining it as a nested compound object each time we use it, we build a custom user type to manage its persistence. A lot of what we need to provide in our custom type is the same as what we put in SourceMediaType (Example 7-1). We'll focus discussion on the new and interesting stuff. Example 7-5 shows one way to persist StereoVolume as a composite user type.

Example 7-5. *StereoVolumeType.java, which is a composite user type to persist StereoVolume*

```
1   package com.oreilly.hh;
2
3   import java.io.Serializable;
4   import java.sql.PreparedStatement;
5   import java.sql.ResultSet;
6   import java.sql.SQLException;
7   import java.sql.Types;
8
9   import net.sf.hibernate.CompositeUserType;
10  import net.sf.hibernate.Hibernate;
11  import net.sf.hibernate.HibernateException;
12  import net.sf.hibernate.engine.SessionImplementor;
13  import net.sf.hibernate.type.Type;
14
15  /**
16   * Manages persistence for the {@link StereoVolume} composite type.
17   */
```

Example 7-5. *StereoVolumeType.java*, which is a composite user type to persist
StereoVolume (continued)

```
18   public class StereoVolumeType implements CompositeUserType {
19
20       /**
21        * Get the names of the properties that make up this composite type,
22        * and that may be used in a query involving it.
23        */
24       public String[] getPropertyNames() {
25           // Allocate a new response each time, because arrays are mutable
26           return new String[] { "left", "right" };
27       }
28
29       /**
30        * Get the types associated with the properties that make up this
31        * composite type.
32        *
33        * @return the types of the parameters reported by
34        *          {@link #getPropertynames}, in the same order.
35        */
36       public Type[] getPropertyTypes() {
37           return new Type[] { Hibernate.SHORT, Hibernate.SHORT };
38       }
39
40       /**
41        * Look up the value of one of the properties making up this composite
42        * type.
43        *
44        * @param component a {@link StereoVolume} instance being managed.
45        * @param property the index of the desired property.
46        * @return the corresponding value.
47        * @see #getPropertyNames
48        */
49       public Object getPropertyValue(Object component, int property) {
50           StereoVolume volume = (StereoVolume)component;
51           short result;
52
53           switch (property) {
54
55           case 0:
56               result = volume.getLeft();
57               break;
58
59           case 1:
60               result = volume.getRight();
61               break;
62
63           default:
64               throw new IllegalArgumentException("unknown property: " +
65                                                         property);
66           }
67
```

```
68              return new Short(result);
69          }
70
71          /**
72           * Set the value of one of the properties making up this composite
73           * type.
74           *
75           * @param component a {@link StereoVolume} instance being managed.
76           * @param property the index of the desired property.
77           * @object value the new value to be established.
78           * @see #getPropertyNames
79           */
80          public void setPropertyValue(Object component, int property, Object value)
81          {
82              StereoVolume volume = (StereoVolume)component;
83              short newLevel = ((Short)value).shortValue();
84              switch (property) {
85
86              case 0:
87                  volume.setLeft(newLevel);
88                  break;
89
90              case 1:
91                  volume.setRight(newLevel);
92                  break;
93
94              default:
95                  throw new IllegalArgumentException("unknown property: " +
96                                                    property);
97              }
98          }
99
100         /**
101          * Determine the class that is returned by {@link #nullSafeGet}.
102          *
103          * @return {@link StereoVolume}, the actual type returned
104          * by {@link #nullSafeGet}.
105          */
106         public Class returnedClass() {
107             return StereoVolume.class;
108         }
109
110         /**
111          * Compare two instances of the class mapped by this type for persistence
112          * "equality".
113          *
114          * @param x first object to be compared.
115          * @param y second object to be compared.
116          * @return <code>true</code> iff both represent the same volume levels.
117          * @throws ClassCastException if x or y isn't a {@link StereoVolume}.
118          */
```

```
119     public boolean equals(Object x, Object y) {
120         if (x == y) {  // This is a trivial success
121             return true;
122         }
123         if (x == null || y == null) {  // Don't blow up if either is null!
124             return false;
125         }
126         // Now it's safe to delegate to the class' own sense of equality
127         return ((StereoVolume)x).equals(y);
128     }
129
130     /**
131      * Return a deep copy of the persistent state, stopping at
132      * entities and collections.
133      *
134      * @param value the object whose state is to be copied.
135      * @return the same object, since enumeration instances are singletons.
136      * @throws ClassCastException for non {@link StereoVolume} values.
137      */
138     public Object deepCopy(Object value) {
139         if (value == null) return null;
140         StereoVolume volume = (StereoVolume)value;
141         return new StereoVolume(volume.getLeft(), volume.getRight());
142     }
143
144     /**
145      * Indicates whether objects managed by this type are mutable.
146      *
147      * @return <code>true</code>, since {@link StereoVolume} is mutable.
148      */
149     public boolean isMutable() {
150         return true;
151     }
152
153     /**
154      * Retrieve an instance of the mapped class from a JDBC {@link ResultSet}.
155      *
156      * @param rs the results from which the instance should be retrieved.
157      * @param names the columns from which the instance should be retrieved.
158      * @param session, an extension of the normal Hibernate session interface
159      *        that gives you much more access to the internals.
160      * @param owner the entity containing the value being retrieved.
161      * @return the retrieved {@link StereoVolume} value, or <code>null</code>.
162      * @throws HibernateException if there is a problem performing the mapping.
163      * @throws SQLException if there is a problem accessing the database.
164      */
165     public Object nullSafeGet(ResultSet rs, String[] names,
166                             SessionImplementor session, Object owner)
167     throws HibernateException, SQLException
168     {
```

```
169            Short left = (Short) Hibernate.SHORT.nullSafeGet(rs, names[0]);
170            Short right = (Short) Hibernate.SHORT.nullSafeGet(rs, names[1]);
171
172            if (left == null || right == null) {
173                return null;  // We don't have a specified volume for the channels
174            }
175
176            return new StereoVolume(left.shortValue(), right.shortValue());
177        }
178
179        /**
180         * Write an instance of the mapped class to a {@link PreparedStatement},
181         * handling null values.
182         *
183         * @param st a JDBC prepared statement.
184         * @param value the StereoVolume value to write.
185         * @param index the parameter index within the prepared statement at which
186         *        this value is to be written.
187         * @param session, an extension of the normal Hibernate session interface
188         *        that gives you much more access to the internals.
189         * @throws HibernateException if there is a problem performing the mapping.
190         * @throws SQLException if there is a problem accessing the database.
191         */
192        public void nullSafeSet(PreparedStatement st, Object value, int index,
193                                SessionImplementor session)
194            throws HibernateException, SQLException
195        {
196            if (value == null) {
197                Hibernate.SHORT.nullSafeSet(st, null, index);
198                Hibernate.SHORT.nullSafeSet(st, null, index + 1);
199            }
200            else {
201                StereoVolume vol = (StereoVolume)value;
202                Hibernate.SHORT.nullSafeSet(st, new Short(vol.getLeft()), index);
203                Hibernate.SHORT.nullSafeSet(st, new Short(vol.getRight()),
204                                            index + 1);
205            }
206        }
207
208        /**
209         * Reconstitute a working instance of the managed class from the cache.
210         *
211         * @param cached the serializable version that was in the cache.
212         * @param session, an extension of the normal Hibernate session interface
213         *        that gives you much more access to the internals.
214         * @param owner the entity containing the value being retrieved.
215         * @return a copy of the value as a {@link StereoVolume} instance.
216         */
217        public Object assemble(Serializable cached, SessionImplementor session,
218                               Object owner)
219        {
```

Example 7-5. *StereoVolumeType.java, which is a composite user type to persist StereoVolume (continued)*

```
220        // Our value type happens to be serializable, so we have an easy out.
221        return deepCopy(cached);
222    }
223
224    /**
225     * Translate an instance of the managed class into a serializable form to
226     * be stored in the cache.
227     *
228     * @param session, an extension of the normal Hibernate session interface
229     *        that gives you much more access to the internals.
230     * @param value the StereoVolume value to be cached.
231     * @return a serializable copy of the value.
232     */
233    public Serializable disassemble(Object value,
234                                      SessionImplementor session) {
235        return (Serializable) deepCopy(value);
236    }
237 }
```

The getPropertyNames() and getPropertyTypes() methods at lines 20 and 29 are how Hibernate knows the "pieces" that make up the composite type. These are the values that are available when you write HQL queries using the type. In our case they correspond to the properties of the actual StereoVolume class we're persisting, but that isn't required. This is our opportunity, for example, to provide a friendly property interface to some legacy object that wasn't designed for persistence at all.

The translation between the virtual properties provided by the composite user type and the real data on which they are based is handled by the getPropertyValue() and setPropertyValue() methods in lines 40–98. In essence, Hibernate hands us an instance of the type we're supposed to manage, about which it makes no assumptions at all, and says "hey, give me the second property" or "set the first property to this value. " You can see how this lets us do any work needed to add a property interface to old or third-party code. In this case, since we don't actually need that power, the hoops we need to jump through to pass the property manipulation on to the underlying StereoVolume class are just boilerplate.

The next lengthy stretch of code consists of methods we've seen before in Example 7-1. Some of the differences in this version are interesting. Most of the changes have to do with the fact that, unlike SourceMedia, our StereoVolume class is mutable—it contains values that can be changed. So we have to come up with full implementations for some methods we finessed last time: comparing instances in equals() at line 110, and making copies in deepCopy() at line 130.

The actual persistence methods, nullSafeGet() at line 153 and nullSafeSet() at 179, are quite similar to Example 7-1, with one difference we didn't need to exploit. They both have a SessionImplementor parameter, which gives you some really deep access to the gears and pulleys that make Hibernate work. This is only needed for truly complex persistence challenges, and it is well outside the scope of this book. If you need to use SessionImplementor methods, you're doing something quite tricky, and you must have a profound understanding of the architecture of Hibernate. You're essentially writing an extension to the system, and you probably need to study the source code to develop the requisite level of expertise.

Finally, the assemble() method at line 208 and disassemble() at 224 allow custom types to support caching of values that aren't already Serializable. They give our persistence manager a place to copy any important values into another object that is capable of being serialized, using any means necessary. Since it was trivial to make StereoVolume serializable in the first place, we don't need this flexibility either. Our implementation can just make copies of the serializable StereoVolume instances for storing in the cache. (We make copies because, again, our data class is mutable, and it wouldn't do to have cached values mysteriously changing.)

That was a lot of work for a simple value class, but the example is a good starting point for more complicated needs.

All right, we've created this beast, how do we use it? Example 7-6 shows how to enhance the volume property in the Track mapping document to use the new composite type. Let's also take this opportunity to add it to Track's toString() method so we can see it in test output.

Example 7-6. Changes to *Track.hbm.xml* to use StereoVolume

```
...
<property name="volume" type="com.oreilly.hh.StereoVolumeType">
  <meta attribute="field-description">How loud to play the track</meta>
  <meta attribute="use-in-tostring">true</meta>
  <column name="VOL_LEFT"/>
  <column name="VOL_RIGHT"/>
</property>
...
```

Notice again that we supply the name of our custom user type, responsible for managing persistence, rather than the raw type that it is managing. This is just like Example 7-2. Also, our composite type uses two columns to store its data, so we need to supply two column names here.

Now when we regenerate the Java source for Track by running **ant codegen**, we get the results shown in Example 7-7.

Example 7-7. Changes to the generated *Track.java* source

```
...
/** nullable persistent field */
private com.oreilly.hh.StereoVolume volume;
...
/** full constructor */
public Track(String title, String filePath, Date playTime, Date added, com.
oreilly.hh.StereoVolume volume, com.oreilly.hh.SourceMedia sourceMedia, Set
artists, Set comments) {
...
}
...
/**
 * How loud to play the track
 */
public com.oreilly.hh.StereoVolume getVolume() {
    return this.volume;
}

public void setVolume(com.oreilly.hh.StereoVolume volume) {
    this.volume = volume;
}
...
public String toString() {
    return new ToStringBuilder(this)
        .append("id", getId())
        .append("title", getTitle())
        .append("volume", getVolume())
        .append("sourceMedia", getSourceMedia())
        .toString();
}
...
```

At this point we are ready to run **ant schema** to recreate the database tables. Example 7-8 shows the relevant output.

Example 7-8. Creation of the Track schema from the new mapping

```
...
[schemaexport] create table TRACK (
[schemaexport]    TRACK_ID INTEGER NOT NULL IDENTITY,
[schemaexport]    title VARCHAR(255) not null,
[schemaexport]    filePath VARCHAR(255) not null,
[schemaexport]    playTime TIME,
[schemaexport]    added DATE,
[schemaexport]    VOL_LEFT SMALLINT,
[schemaexport]    VOL_RIGHT SMALLINT,
[schemaexport]    sourceMedia VARCHAR(255)
[schemaexport] )
...
```

Let's beef up the data creation test so it can work with the new Track structure. Example 7-9 shows the kind of changes we need.

Example 7-9. *Changes required to CreateTest.java to test stereo volumes*

```
...
// Create some data and persist it
tx = session.beginTransaction();
StereoVolume fullVolume = new StereoVolume();

Track track = new Track("Russian Trance",
                        "vol2/album610/track02.mp3",
                        Time.valueOf("00:03:30"), new Date(),
                        fullVolume, SourceMedia.CD,
                        new HashSet(), new HashSet());
addTrackArtist(track, getArtist("PPK", true, session));
session.save(track);
...
// The other tracks created use fullVolume too, until...
...
track = new Track("Test Tone 1",
                  "vol2/singles/test01.mp3",
                  Time.valueOf("00:00:10"), new Date(),
                  new StereoVolume((short)50, (short)75), null,
                  new HashSet(), new HashSet());
track.getComments().add("Pink noise to test equalization");
session.save(track);
...
```

Now if we execute **ant ctest** and look at the results with **ant db**, we'll find values like those shown in Figure 7-2.

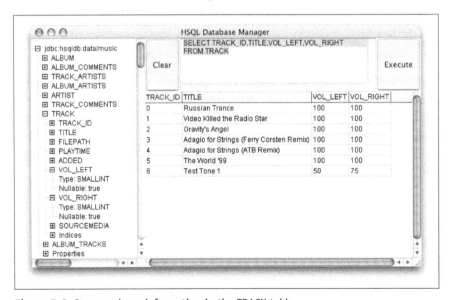

Figure 7-2. *Stereo volume information in the TRACK table*

We only need to make the single change, shown in Example 7-10, to AlbumTest to make it compatible with this new Track format.

Example 7-10. *Change to AlbumTest.java to support stereo track volumes*

```
...
private static void addAlbumTrack(Album album, String title, String file,
                                  Time length, Artist artist, int disc,
                                  int positionOnDisc, Session session)
        throws HibernateException
{
    Track track = new Track(title, file, length, new Date(),
                            new StereoVolume(), SourceMedia.CD,
                            new HashSet(), new HashSet());
    ...
```

This lets us run **ant atest**, and see the stereo volume information shown by the new version of Track's toString() method in Example 7-11.

Example 7-11. *An album with stereo track information*

```
atest:
     [java] com.oreilly.hh.Album@a49182[id=0,title=Counterfeit e.p.,tracks=[com.
oreilly.hh.AlbumTrack@548719[track=com.oreilly.hh.Track@719d5b[id=<null>,
title=Compulsion,volume=Volume[left=100, right=100],sourceMedia=Compact Disc]],
com.oreilly.hh.AlbumTrack@afebc9[track=com.oreilly.hh.Track@a0fbd6[id=<null>,
title=In a Manner of Speaking,volume=Volume[left=100,
right=100],sourceMedia=Compact Disc]], com.oreilly.hh.
AlbumTrack@f5c8fb[track=com.oreilly.hh.Track@5dfb22[id=<null>,title=Smile in the
Crowd,volume=Volume[left=100, right=100],sourceMedia=Compact Disc]], com.oreilly.
hh.AlbumTrack@128f03[track=com.oreilly.hh.Track@6b2ab7[id=<null>,
title=Gone,volume=Volume[left=100, right=100],sourceMedia=Compact Disc]], com.
oreilly.hh.AlbumTrack@c17a8c[track=com.oreilly.hh.Track@549f0e[id=<null>,
title=Never Turn Your Back on Mother Earth,volume=Volume[left=100,
right=100],sourceMedia=Compact Disc]], com.oreilly.hh.
AlbumTrack@9652dd[track=com.oreilly.hh.Track@1a67fe[id=<null>,title=Motherless
Child,volume=Volume[left=100, right=100],sourceMedia=Compact Disc]]]]
```

Well, that may have been more in-depth than you wanted right now about creating custom types, but someday you might come back and mine this example for the exact nugget you're looking for. In the meantime, let's change gears and look at something new, simple, and completely different. The next chapter introduces criteria queries, a unique and very programmer-friendly capability in Hibernate.

Phew!

## CHAPTER 8

Criteria Queries

Relational query languages like HQL (and SQL, on which it's based) are extremely flexible and powerful, but they take a long time to truly master. Many application developers get by with a rudimentary understanding, cribbing similar examples from past projects, and calling in database experts when they need to come up with something truly new, or to understand a particularly cryptic query expression.

It can also be awkward to mix a query language's syntax with Java code. The section "Better Ways to Build Queries" in Chapter 3 showed how to at least keep the queries in a separate file so they can be seen and edited in one piece, free of Java string escape sequences and concatenation syntax. Even with that technique, though, the HQL isn't parsed until the mapping document is loaded, which means that any syntax errors it might harbor won't be caught until the application is running.

Hibernate offers an unusual solution to these problems in the form of criteria queries. They provide a way to create and connect simple Java objects that act as filters for picking your desired results. You can build up nested, structured expressions. The mechanism also allows you to supply example objects to show what you're looking for, with control over which details matter and which properties to ignore.

As you'll see, this can be quite convenient. To be fair, it has its own disadvantages. Expanding long query expressions into a Java API makes them take more room, and they'll be less familiar to experienced database developers than a SQL-like query. There are also some things you simply can't express using the current criteria API, such as *projection* (retrieving a subset of the properties of a class, e.g., "select title, id from com.oreilly.hh.Track" rather than "select * from com.oreilly. hh.Track") and *aggregation* (summarizing results, e.g., getting the sum, average, or count of a property). The next chapter shows how to accomplish such tasks using Hibernate's object-oriented query language.

In this chapter:
- *Using Simple Criteria*
- *Compounding Criteria*
- *Applying Criteria to Associations*
- *Querying by Example*

Using Simple Criteria

Let's start by building a criteria query to find tracks shorter than a specified length, replacing the HQL we used in Example 3-9 and updating the code of Example 3-10.

How do I do that?

The first thing we need to figure out is how to specify the kind of object we're interested in retrieving. There is no query language involved in building criteria queries. Instead, you build up a tree of `Criteria` objects describing what you want. The Hibernate `Session` acts as a factory for these criteria, and you start, conveniently enough, by specifying the type of objects you want to retrieve.

Edit *QueryTest.java*, replacing the contents of the `tracksNoLongerThan()` method with those shown in Example 8-1.

Example 8-1. The beginnings of a criteria query

```
public static List tracksNoLongerThan(Time length, Session session)
    throws HibernateException
{
    Criteria criteria = session.createCriteria(Track.class);
    return criteria.list();
}
```

These examples assume the database has been set up as described in the preceding chapters. If you don't want to go through all that, download the sample code, then jump into this chapter and run the "codegen", "schema", and "ctest" targets.

The session's `createCriteria()` method builds a criteria query that will return instances of the persistent class you supply as an argument. Easy enough. If you run the example at this point, of course, you'll see all the tracks in the database, since we haven't gotten around to expressing any actual *criteria* to limit our results yet (Example 8-2).

Example 8-2. Our fledgling criteria query returns all tracks

```
% ant qtest
...
qtest:
     [java] Track: "Russian Trance" (PPK) 00:03:30, from Compact Disc
     [java] Track: "Video Killed the Radio Star" (The Buggles) 00:03:49, from VHS
Videocassette Tape
     [java] Track: "Gravity's Angel" (Laurie Anderson) 00:06:06, from Compact Disc
     [java] Track: "Adagio for Strings (Ferry Corsten Remix)" (Ferry Corsten,
William Orbit, Samuel Barber) 00:06:35, from Compact Disc
     [java] Track: "Adagio for Strings (ATB Remix)" (ATB, William Orbit, Samuel
Barber) 00:07:39, from Compact Disc
     [java] Track: "The World '99" (Ferry Corsten, Pulp Victim) 00:07:05, from
Digital Audio Stream
     [java] Track: "Test Tone 1" 00:00:10
     [java]    Comment: Pink noise to test equalization
```

OK, easy enough. How about picking the tracks we want? Also easy! Add a new import statement at the top of the file:

```
import net.sf.hibernate.expression.*;
```

Then just add one more line to the method, as in Example 8-3.

Example 8-3. The criteria query that fully replaces the HQL version from Chapter 3

```
public static List tracksNoLongerThan(Time length, Session session)
    throws HibernateException
{
    Criteria criteria = session.createCriteria(Track.class);
    criteria.add(Expression.le("playTime", length));
    return criteria.list();
}
```

The Expression class acts as a factory for obtaining Criterion instances that can specify different kinds of constraints on your query. Its le() method creates a criterion that constrains a property to be less than or equal to a specified value. In this case we want the Track's playTime property to be no greater than the value passed in to the method. We add this to our set of desired criteria.

Just like HQL, expressions are always in terms of object properties, not table columns.

We'll look at some other Criterion types available through Expression in the next section. Appendix B lists them all, and you can create your own implementations of the Criterion interface if you've got something new you want to support.

Running the query this time gives us just the tracks that are no more than seven minutes long, as requested by the main() method (Example 8-4).

Example 8-4. Results of our complete simple criteria query

```
% ant qtest
...
qtest:
    [java] Track: "Russian Trance" (PPK) 00:03:30, from Compact Disc
    [java] Track: "Video Killed the Radio Star" (The Buggles) 00:03:49, from VHS
Videocassette Tape
    [java] Track: "Gravity's Angel" (Laurie Anderson) 00:06:06, from Compact Disc
    [java] Track: "Adagio for Strings (Ferry Corsten Remix)" (Ferry Corsten,
William Orbit, Samuel Barber) 00:06:35, from Compact Disc
    [java] Track: "Test Tone 1" 00:00:10
    [java]    Comment: Pink noise to test equalization
```

A surprising number of the queries used to retrieve objects in real applications are very simple, and criteria queries are an extremely natural and compact way of expressing them in Java. Our new tracksNoLongerThan() method is actually shorter than it was in

Example 3-10, and that version required a separate query (Example 3-9) to be added to the mapping document as well! Both approaches lead to the same patterns of underlying database access, so they are equally efficient at runtime.

In fact, you can make the code even more compact. The add() and createCriteria() methods return the Criteria instance, so you can continue to manipulate it in the same Java statement. Taking advantage of that, we can boil the method down to the version in Example 8-5.

Example 8-5. An even more compact version of our criteria query

```
public static List tracksNoLongerThan(Time length, Session session)
    throws HibernateException
{
    return session.createCriteria(Track.class).
        add(Expression.le("playTime", length)).list();
}
```

The style you choose is a trade-off between space and readability (although some people may find the compact, run-on version even more readable). Even though this is marked as an experimental API, it already looks extremely useful, and I expect to adopt it in many places.

What about...

...Sorting the list of results, or retrieving a subset of all matching objects? Like the Query interface, the Criteria interface lets you limit the number of results you get back (and choose where to start) by calling setMaxResults() and setFirstResult(). It also lets you control the order in which they're returned (which you'd do using an order by clause in an HQL query), as shown in Example 8-6.

Example 8-6. Sorting the results by title

```
public static List tracksNoLongerThan(Time length, Session session)
    throws HibernateException
{
    Criteria criteria = session.createCriteria(Track.class);
    criteria.add(Expression.le("playTime", length));
    criteria.addOrder(Order.asc("title"));
    return criteria.list();
}
```

The Order class is just a way of representing orderings. It has two static factory methods, asc() and desc(), for creating ascending or descending orderings respectively. Each takes the name of the property to be sorted. The results of running this version are in Example 8-7.

Example 8-7. The sorted results

```
% ant qtest
...
qtest:
    [java] Track: "Adagio for Strings (Ferry Corsten Remix)" (Ferry Corsten,
William Orbit, Samuel Barber) 00:06:35, from Compact Disc
    [java] Track: "Gravity's Angel" (Laurie Anderson) 00:06:06, from Compact Disc
    [java] Track: "Russian Trance" (PPK) 00:03:30, from Compact Disc
    [java] Track: "Test Tone 1" 00:00:10
    [java]    Comment: Pink noise to test equalization
    [java] Track: "Video Killed the Radio Star" (The Buggles) 00:03:49, from VHS
Videocassette Tape
```

You can add more than one Order to the Criteria, and it will sort by each of them in turn (the first gets priority, and then if there are any results with the same value for that property, the second ordering is applied to them, and so on).

Compounding Criteria

As you might expect, you can add more than one Criterion to your query, and all of them must be satisfied for objects to be included in the results. This is equivalent to building a compound criterion using Expression.conjunction(), as described in Appendix B. As in Example 8-8, we can restrict our results so that the tracks also have to contain a capital "A" somewhere in their title by adding another line to our method.

Example 8-8. A pickier list of short tracks

```
Criteria criteria = session.createCriteria(Track.class);
criteria.add(Expression.le("playTime", length));
criteria.add(Expression.like("title", "%A%"));
criteria.addOrder(Order.asc("title"));
return criteria.list();
```

With this in place, we get fewer results (Example 8-9).

Example 8-9. Tracks of seven minutes or less containing a capital A in their titles

```
qtest:
    [java] Track: "Adagio for Strings (Ferry Corsten Remix)" (Ferry Corsten,
William Orbit, Samuel Barber) 00:06:35, from Compact Disc
    [java] Track: "Gravity's Angel" (Laurie Anderson) 00:06:06, from Compact Disc
```

If you want to find any objects matching any one of your criteria, rather than requiring them to fit all criteria, you need to explicitly use Expression.disjunction() to group them. You can build up combinations of such groupings, and other complex hierarchies, using the built-in criteria offered by the Expression class. Check Appendix B for the details. Example 8-10 shows how we'd change the sample query to give us tracks that *either* met the length restriction or contained a capital A.

Example 8-10. Picking tracks more leniently

```
Criteria criteria = session.createCriteria(Track.class);
Disjunction any = Expression.disjunction();
any.add(Expression.le("playTime", length));
any.add(Expression.like("title", "%A%"));
criteria.add(any);
criteria.addOrder(Order.asc("title"));
        return criteria.list();
```

This results in us picking up a new version of "Adagio for Strings" (Example 8-11).

Example 8-11. Tracks whose title contains the letter A, or whose length is seven minutes or less

```
qtest:
    [java] Track: "Adagio for Strings (ATB Remix)" (ATB, William Orbit, Samuel
Barber) 00:07:39, from Compact Disc
    [java] Track: "Adagio for Strings (Ferry Corsten Remix)" (Ferry Corsten,
William Orbit, Samuel Barber) 00:06:35, from Compact Disc
    [java] Track: "Gravity's Angel" (Laurie Anderson) 00:06:06, from Compact Disc
    [java] Track: "Russian Trance" (PPK) 00:03:30, from Compact Disc
    [java] Track: "Test Tone 1" 00:00:10
    [java]    Comment: Pink noise to test equalization
    [java] Track: "Video Killed the Radio Star" (The Buggles) 00:03:49, from VHS
Videocassette Tape
```

Finally, note that it's still possible, thanks to the clever return values of these methods, to consolidate our method into a single expression (Example 8-12).

Example 8-12. Taking code compactness a bit too far

```
return session.createCriteria(Track.class).add(Expression.disjunction().
 add(Expression.le("playTime", length)).add(Expression.like("title", "%A%"))).
 addOrder(Order.asc("title")).list();
```

Although this yields the same results, I hope you agree it doesn't do good things for the readability of the method (except perhaps to LISP experts)!

You can use the facilities in Expression to build up a wide variety of multi-part criteria. Some things still require HQL, and past a certain threshold of complexity, you're probably better off in that environment. But you can do a lot with criteria queries, and they're often the right way to go.

Applying Criteria to Associations

So far we've been looking at the properties of a single class in forming our criteria. Of course, in our real systems, we've got a rich set of associations between objects, and sometimes the details we want to use to filter our results come from these associations. Fortunately, the criteria query API provides a straightforward way of performing such searches.

How do I do that?

Let's suppose we're interested in finding all the tracks associated with particular artists. We'd want our criteria to look at the values contained in each Track's artists property, which is a collection of associations to Artist objects. Just to make it a bit more fun, let's say we want to be able to find tracks associated with artists whose name property matches a particular SQL string pattern.

Let's add a new method to *QueryTest.java* to implement this. Add the method shown in Example 8-13 after the end of the tracksNoLongerThan() method.

Example 8-13. Filtering tracks based on their artist associations

```
 1  /**
 2   * Retrieve any tracks associated with artists whose name matches a
 3   * SQL string pattern.
 4   *
 5   * @param namePattern the pattern which an artist's name must match
 6   * @param session the Hibernate session that can retrieve data.
 7   * @return a list of {@link Track}s meeting the artist name restriction.
 8   * @throws HibernateException if there is a problem.
 9   */
10  public static List tracksWithArtistLike(String namePattern, Session session)
11      throws HibernateException
12  {
13      Criteria criteria = session.createCriteria(Track.class);
14      Criteria artistCriteria = criteria.createCriteria("artists");
15      artistCriteria.add(Expression.like("name", namePattern));
16      criteria.addOrder(Order.asc("title"));
17      return criteria.list();
18  }
```

Line 14 creates a second Criteria instance, attached to the one we're using to select tracks, by following the tracks' artists property. We can add constraints to either criteria (which would apply to the properties of the Track itself), or to artistCriteria, which causes them to apply to the properties of the `Artist` entities associated with the track. In this case, we are only interested in features of the artists, so line 15 restricts our results to tracks associated with at least one artist whose name matches the specified pattern. (By applying constraints to both `Criteria`, we could restrict by both `Track` and `Artist` properties.)

Line 16 requests sorting on the tracks we get back, so we'll see the results in alphabetical order. In the current implementation of criteria queries, you can only sort the outermost criteria, not the subcriteria you create for associations. If you try, you'll be rewarded with an `UnsupportedOperationException`.

At least its error message is helpful and descriptive!

To see all this in action, we need to make one more change. Modify the `main()` method so that it invokes this new query, as shown in Example 8-14.

Example 8-14. Calling the new track artist name query

```
...
// Ask for a session using the JDBC information we've configured
Session session = sessionFactory.openSession();
try {
    // Print tracks associated with an artist whose name ends with "n"
    List tracks = tracksWithArtistLike("%n", session);
    for (ListIterator iter = tracks.listIterator() ;
...
```

Running **ant qtest** now gives the results shown in Example 8-15.

Example 8-15. Tracks associated with an artist whose name ends with the letter n

```
qtest:
     [java] Track: "Adagio for Strings (Ferry Corsten Remix)" (Ferry Corsten,
William Orbit, Samuel Barber) 00:06:35, from Compact Disc
     [java] Track: "Gravity's Angel" (Laurie Anderson) 00:06:06, from Compact Disc
     [java] Track: "The World '99" (Ferry Corsten, Pulp Victim) 00:07:05, from
Digital Audio Stream
```

What just happened?

If you look at the lists of artists for each of the three tracks that were found, you'll see that at least one of them has a name ending in "n" as we requested. Also notice that we have access to all the artists associated with each track, not just the ones that matched the name criterion. This is what you'd expect and want, given that we've retrieved the actual `Track` entities. You can run criteria queries in a different mode, by calling `setResultTransformer(Criteria.ALIAS_TO_ENTITY_MAP)`, which causes it to return a list of hierarchical `Maps` in which the criteria at each level have filtered the results. This goes beyond the scope of this notebook, but there are some examples of it in the reference and API documentation.

You can also create aliases for the associations you're working with, and use those aliases in expressions. This starts getting complex but it's useful. Explore it someday.

TIP

If the table from which you're fetching objects might contain duplicate entries, you can achieve the equivalent of SQL's "select distinct" by calling setResultTransformer(Criteria. DISTINCT_ROOT_ENTITY) on your criteria.

Querying by Example

If you don't want to worry about setting up expressions and criteria, but you've got an object that shows what you're looking for, you can use it as an example and have Hibernate build the criteria for you.

How do I do that?

Let's add another query method to *QueryTest.java*. Add the code of Example 8-16 to the top of the class where the other queries are.

Example 8-16. Using an example entity to populate a criteria query

```
1   /**
2    * Retrieve any tracks that were obtained from a particular source
3    * media type.
4    *
5    * @param sourceMedia the media type of interest.
6    * @param session the Hibernate session that can retrieve data.
7    * @return a list of {@link Track}s meeting the media restriction.
8    * @throws HibernateException if there is a problem.
9    */
10  public static List tracksFromMedia(SourceMedia media, Session session)
11          throws HibernateException
12  {
13      Track track = new Track();
14      track.setSourceMedia(media);
15      Example example = Example.create(track);
16
17      Criteria criteria = session.createCriteria(Track.class);
18      criteria.add(example);
19      criteria.addOrder(Order.asc("title"));
20      return criteria.list();
21  }
```

Lines 13 and 14 create the example Track and set the sourceMedia property to represent what we're looking for. Line 15 wraps it in an Example object. This object gives you some control over which properties will be used in building criteria and how strings are matched. The default behavior is that null properties are ignored, and that strings are compared in a case-sensitive and literal way. You can call example's excludeZeroes() method if you want properties with a value of zero to be ignored too, or excludeNone() if even null properties are to be matched. An excludeProperty() method lets you explicitly ignore specific properties by name, but that's starting to get a lot like building criteria by hand. To tune string handling, there are ignoreCase() and enableLike() methods, which do just what they sound like.

Line 17 creates a criteria query, just like our other examples in this chapter, but we then add our example to it instead of using Expression to create a criterion. Hibernate takes care of translating example into the corresponding criteria. Lines 19 and 20 are just like our previous query methods: setting up a sort order, running the query, and returning the list of matching entities.

Once again we need to modify the main() method to call our new query. Let's find the tracks that came from CDs. Make the changes shown in Example 8-17.

Example 8-17. Changes to main() to call our example-driven query method

```
...
// Ask for a session using the JDBC information we've configured
Session session = sessionFactory.openSession();
try {
    // Print tracks that came from CDs
    List tracks = tracksFromMedia(SourceMedia.CD, session);
    for (ListIterator iter = tracks.listIterator() ;
...
```

Running this version produces output like Example 8-18.

Example 8-18. Results of querying by example for tracks from CDs

```
qtest:
    [java] Track: "Adagio for Strings (ATB Remix)" (ATB, William Orbit, Samuel
Barber) 00:07:39, from Compact Disc
    [java] Track: "Adagio for Strings (Ferry Corsten Remix)" (Ferry Corsten,
William Orbit, Samuel Barber) 00:06:35, from Compact Disc
    [java] Track: "Gravity's Angel" (Laurie Anderson) 00:06:06, from Compact Disc
    [java] Track: "Russian Trance" (PPK) 00:03:30, from Compact Disc
```

As you might expect, you can use examples with subcriteria for associated objects, too. We could rewrite tracksWithArtistLike() so that it uses an example Artist rather than building its criterion "by hand." We'll need to call enableLike() on our example. Example 8-19 shows a concise way of doing this.

Example 8-19. Updating the artist name query to use an example artist

```
public static List tracksWithArtistLike(String namePattern, Session session)
    throws HibernateException
{
    Criteria criteria = session.createCriteria(Track.class);
    Example example = Example.create(new Artist(namePattern, null, null));
    criteria.createCriteria("artists").add(example.enableLike());
    criteria.addOrder(Order.asc("title"));
    return criteria.list();
}
```

Remember that if you want to try running this you'll need to switch main() back to the way it was in Example 8-14.

A great variety of queries that power the user interface and general operation of a typical data-driven Java application can be expressed as criteria queries, and they provide advantages in readability, compile-time type checking, and even (surprisingly) compactness. As far as experimental APIs go, I'd call this a winner.

When criteria queries don't quite do the job, you can turn to the full power of HQL, which we'll investigate in the next chapter.

Criteria queries are pretty neat, aren't they? I like them a lot more than I expected.

## CHAPTER 9

A Look at HQL

HQL queries have already been used a few times in previous chapters. It's worth spending a little time looking at how HQL differs from SQL and some of the useful things you can do with it. As with the rest of this notebook, our intention is to provide a useful introduction and some examples, not a comprehensive reference.

Writing HQL Queries

We've already shown that you can get by with fewer pieces in an HQL query than you might be used to in SQL (the queries we've been using, such as those in Chapter 3, have generally omitted the "select" clause). In fact, the only thing you really *need* to specify is the class in which you're interested. Example 9-1 shows a minimal query that's a perfectly valid way to get a list of all Track instances persisted in the database.

Example 9-1. The simplest HQL query

```
from Track
```

HQL stands for Hibernate Query Language. And SQL? It depends who you ask.

There's not much to it, is there? This is the HQL equivalent of Example 8-1, in which we built a criteria query on the Track class and supplied no criteria.

By default, Hibernate automatically "imports" the names of each class you map, which means you don't have to provide a fully qualified package name when you want to use it, the simple class name is enough. As long as you've not mapped more than one class with the same name, you don't need to use fully qualified class names in your queries. You are certainly free to do so if you prefer—as I have in this book to help readers remember that the queries are expressed in terms of Java data beans and their properties, *not* database tables and columns (like you'd find in SQL). Example 9-2 produces precisely the same result as our first query.

Example 9-2. Explicit package naming, but still pretty simple

```
from com.oreilly.hh.Track
```

If you do have more than one mapped class with the same name, you can either use the fully qualified package name to refer to each, or you can assign an alternate name for one or both classes using an import tag in their mapping documents. You can also turn off the auto-import facility for a mapping file by adding auto-import="false" to the hibernate-mapping tag's attributes.

TIP

You're probably used to queries being case-insensitive, since SQL behaves this way. For the most part, HQL acts the same, with the important exceptions of class and property names. Just as in the rest of Java, these are case-sensitive, so you must get the capitalization right.

Let's look at an extreme example of how HQL differs from SQL, by pushing its polymorphic query capability to its logical limit.

How do I do that?

A powerful way to highlight the fundamental difference between SQL and HQL is to consider what happens when you query "from java.lang.Object". At first glance this might not even seem to make sense! In fact, Hibernate supports queries that return polymorphic results. If you've got mapped classes that extend each other, or have some shared ancestor or interface, whether you've mapped the classes to the same table or to different tables, you can query the superclass. Since every Java object extends Object, this query asks Hibernate to return every single entity it knows about in the database.

We can test this by making a quick variant of our query test. Copy *QueryTest.java* to *QueryTest3.java*, and make the changes shown in Example 9-3 (most of the changes, which don't show up in the example, involve deleting example queries we don't need here).

Example 9-3. Look, Toto, we're not in SQL anymore

```
1  package com.oreilly.hh;
2
3  import net.sf.hibernate.*;
4  import net.sf.hibernate.cfg.Configuration;
5
6  import java.util.*;
7
8  /**
9   * Retrieve all persistent objects
10  */
11 public class QueryTest3 {
12
13    /**
14     * Look up and print all entities when invoked from the command line.
15     */
16    public static void main(String args[]) throws Exception {
17        // Create a configuration based on the properties file we've put
18        // in the standard place.
19        Configuration config = new Configuration();
20
21        // Tell it about the classes we want mapped, taking advantage of
22        // the way we've named their mapping documents.
23        config.addClass(Track.class).addClass(Artist.class);
24        config.addClass(Album.class);
25
26        // Get the session factory we can use for persistence
27        SessionFactory sessionFactory = config.buildSessionFactory();
28
29        // Ask for a session using the JDBC information we've configured
30        Session session = sessionFactory.openSession();
31        try {
32            // Print every mapped object in the database
33            List all = session.find("from java.lang.Object");
34            for (ListIterator iter = all.listIterator() ;
35                 iter.hasNext() ; ) {
36                System.out.println(iter.next());
37            }
38        } finally {
39            // No matter what, close the session
40            session.close();
41        }
42
43        // Clean up after ourselves
44        sessionFactory.close();
45    }
46 }
```

We added line 24 because Hibernate will only return objects whose mappings it has been asked to load, and we'd like to see everything we can put in the database. To be sure you've got all the sample data created, run **ant schema ctest atest**. Line 33 invokes the odd and powerful query, and line 36 prints what we've found. We can't do much more than call toString() on the objects we get back because we don't know what they might be. Object is not very deep as a shared interface.

There's one more step we need to take before we can run this. Add another target to *build.xml,* as shown in Example 9-4.

Example 9-4. Invoking the über-query

```
<target name="qtest3" description="Retrieve all mapped objects"
        depends="compile">
  <java classname="com.oreilly.hh.QueryTest3" fork="true">
    <classpath refid="project.class.path"/>
  </java>
</target>
```

Then you can test it by running **ant   qtest3**. You'll see results like Example 9-5.

Example 9-5. Everything Hibernate can find

```
% ant qtest3
Buildfile: build.xml

prepare:

compile:
    [javac] Compiling 1 source file to /Users/jim/Documents/Work/OReilly/
Hibernate/Examples/ch09/classes

qtest3:
    [java] com.oreilly.hh.Album@397cea[id=0,title=Counterfeit e.p.,tracks=[com.
oreilly.hh.AlbumTrack@5e60f2[track=com.oreilly.hh.
Track@aaa10[id=7,title=Compulsion,sourceMedia=Compact Disc]], com.oreilly.hh.
AlbumTrack@2ed1e8[track=com.oreilly.hh.Track@231e35[id=8,title=In a Manner of
Speaking,sourceMedia=Compact Disc]], com.oreilly.hh.AlbumTrack@d6f84a[track=com.
oreilly.hh.Track@9432e0[id=9,title=Smile in the Crowd,sourceMedia=Compact Disc]],
com.oreilly.hh.AlbumTrack@46ca65[track=com.oreilly.hh.
Track@9830bc[id=10,title=Gone,sourceMedia=Compact Disc]], com.oreilly.hh.
AlbumTrack@91e365[track=com.oreilly.hh.Track@a79447[id=11,title=Never Turn Your
Back on Mother Earth,sourceMedia=Compact Disc]], com.oreilly.hh.
AlbumTrack@e823ac[track=com.oreilly.hh.Track@f801c4[id=12,title=Motherless
Child,sourceMedia=Compact Disc]]]]
    [java] com.oreilly.hh.Artist@e7736c[id=0,name=PPK,actualArtist=<null>]
    [java] com.oreilly.hh.Artist@a59727[id=1,name=The
Buggles,actualArtist=<null>]
    [java] com.oreilly.hh.Artist@1f7fbe[id=2,name=Laurie
Anderson,actualArtist=<null>]
    [java] com.oreilly.hh.Artist@f42d53[id=3,name=William
Orbit,actualArtist=<null>]
    [java] com.oreilly.hh.Artist@ba63a2[id=4,name=Ferry
Corsten,actualArtist=<null>]
    [java] com.oreilly.hh.Artist@e668c2[id=5,name=Samuel
Barber,actualArtist=<null>]
```

As usual, these examples assume you've set up the environment by following the preceding chapters. You can also just use the downloadable sample source for this chapter.

Example 9-5. *Everything Hibernate can find (continued)*

```
    [java] com.oreilly.hh.Artist@d67d61[id=6,name=ATB,actualArtist=<null>]
    [java] com.oreilly.hh.Artist@e9a555[id=7,name=Pulp
Victim,actualArtist=<null>]
    [java] com.oreilly.hh.Artist@6a4aef[id=8,name=Martin L.
Gore,actualArtist=<null>]
    [java] com.oreilly.hh.Track@4dba7f[id=0,title=Russian
Trance,sourceMedia=Compact Disc]
    [java] com.oreilly.hh.Track@906563[id=1,title=Video Killed the Radio
Star,sourceMedia=VHS Videocassette Tape]
    [java] com.oreilly.hh.Track@f068b9[id=2,title=Gravity's
Angel,sourceMedia=Compact Disc]
    [java] com.oreilly.hh.Track@6b54ef[id=3,title=Adagio for Strings (Ferry
Corsten Remix),sourceMedia=Compact Disc]
    [java] com.oreilly.hh.Track@954549[id=4,title=Adagio for Strings (ATB
Remix),sourceMedia=Compact Disc]
    [java] com.oreilly.hh.Track@f7dab1[id=5,title=The World
'99,sourceMedia=Digital Audio Stream]
    [java] com.oreilly.hh.Track@36d1d7[id=6,title=Test Tone 1,sourceMedia=<null>]
    [java] com.oreilly.hh.Track@aaa10[id=7,title=Compulsion,sourceMedia=Compact
Disc]
    [java] com.oreilly.hh.Track@231e35[id=8,title=In a Manner of
Speaking,sourceMedia=Compact Disc]
    [java] com.oreilly.hh.Track@9432e0[id=9,title=Smile in the
Crowd,sourceMedia=Compact Disc]
    [java] com.oreilly.hh.Track@9830bc[id=10,title=Gone,sourceMedia=Compact
Disc]
    [java] com.oreilly.hh.Track@a79447[id=11,title=Never Turn Your Back on Mother
Earth,sourceMedia=Compact Disc]
    [java] com.oreilly.hh.Track@f801c4[id=12,title=Motherless
Child,sourceMedia=Compact Disc]

BUILD SUCCESSFUL
Total time: 17 seconds
```

What just happened?

Well, it's pretty remarkable if you think about it, because Hibernate had to do several separate SQL queries in order to obtain the results for us. A whole lot of work went on behind the scenes to hand us that list of every known persisted entity. Although it's hard to imagine a situation where you'll actually need to do something exactly like this, it certainly highlights some of the interesting capabilities of HQL and Hibernate.

And there are certainly times when slightly less comprehensive queries will be very useful to you, so it's worth keeping in mind that table-spanning polymorphic queries are not only possible, but easy to use.

There are some limitations that come into play when you run an HQL query that requires multiple separate SQL queries to implement. You can't use order by clauses to sort the entire set of results, nor can you use the Query interface's scroll() method to walk through them.

What about...

...Associations and joins? These are easy to work with as well. You can traverse associations by simply following the property chain, using periods as delimiters. To help you refer to a particular entity in your query expressions, HQL lets you assign aliases, just like SQL. This is particularly important if you want to refer to two separate entities of the same class, for example:

```
from com.oreilly.hh.Track as track1
```

which is equivalent to

```
from com.oreilly.hh.Track track1
```

The version you'll use will most likely depend on what you're used to, or the style guidelines established for your project.

We'll see examples of joins below, once we introduce enough other HQL elements to make them interesting.

Selecting Properties and Pieces

The queries we've been using so far have returned entire persistent objects. This is the most common use of an object/relational mapping service like Hibernate, so it should come as no surprise. Once you've got the objects, you can use them in whatever way you need to within the familiar realm of Java code. There are circumstances where you might want only a subset of the properties that make up an object, though, such as producing reports. HQL can accommodate such needs, in exactly the same way you'd use ordinary SQL—projection in a select clause.

How do I do that?

Suppose we want to change *QueryTest.java* to display only the titles of the tracks that meet our search criteria, and we want to extract only that information from the database in the first place. We'd start by changing the query of Example 3-9 to retrieve only the title property. Edit *Track.hbm.xml* to make the query look like Example 9-6.

Example 9-6. Obtaining just the titles of the short tracks

```
<query name="com.oreilly.hh.tracksNoLongerThan">
  <![CDATA[
      select track.title from com.oreilly.hh.Track as track
      where track.playTime <= :length
  ]]>
</query>
```

Make sure the tracksNoLongerThan() method in *QueryTest.java* is set up to use this query. (If you edited it to use criteria queries in Chapter 8, change it back to the way it was in Example 3-10. To save you the trouble of hunting that down, it's reproduced as Example 9-7.)

Example 9-7. HQL-driven query method, using the query mapped in Example 9-6

```
public static List tracksNoLongerThan(Time length, Session session)
    throws HibernateException
{
    Query query = session.getNamedQuery(
                    "com.oreilly.hh.tracksNoLongerThan");
    query.setTime("length", length);
    return query.list();
}
```

Finally, the main() method needs to be updated, as shown in Example 9-8, to reflect the fact that the query method is now returning the title property rather than entire Track records. This property is defined as a String, so the method now returns a List of Strings.

Example 9-8. Changes to QueryTest's main() method to work with the title query

```
// Print the titles of tracks that will fit in five minutes
List titles = tracksNoLongerThan(Time.valueOf("00:05:00"),
                                 session);
for (ListIterator iter = titles.listIterator() ;
    iter.hasNext() ; ) {
    String aTitle = (String)iter.next();
    System.out.println("Track: " + aTitle);
}
```

Those changes are pretty simple, and the relationship between the return type of the query and the list elements we see in Java is straightforward. Depending on what data you've set up, running this version using **ant qtest** will result in output similar to Example 9-9. (If you've not got any data, or you want it to look just like this, recreate the test data before displaying it by running **ant schema ctest atest qtest**.)

Example 9-9. Listing just the titles of tracks no more than five minutes long

```
qtest:
     [java] Track: Russian Trance
     [java] Track: Video Killed the Radio Star
     [java] Track: Test Tone 1
     [java] Track: In a Manner of Speaking
     [java] Track: Gone
     [java] Track: Never Turn Your Back on Mother Earth
     [java] Track: Motherless Child
```

What about...

...Returning more than one property? You can certainly do this, and the properties can come from multiple objects if you're using a join, or if your query object has components or associations (which are, after all, a very convenient form of object-oriented join). As you'd expect from SQL, all you do is list the properties you'd like, separated by commas. As a simple example, let's get the IDs as well as the titles for our tracks in this query. Tweak *Track.hbm.xml* so the query looks like Example 9-10.

Example 9-10. Selecting multiple properties from an object

```
<query name="com.oreilly.hh.tracksNoLongerThan">
  <![CDATA[
      select track.id, track.title from com.oreilly.hh.Track as track
      where track.playTime <= :length
  ]]>
</query>
```

We don't need to change the query method at all; it still invokes this query by name, passes in the same named parameter, and returns the resulting list. But what does that list contain now? We'll need to update our loop in main() so that it can show both the IDs and the titles.

In situations like this, when it needs to return multiple, separate values for each "row" in a query, each entry in the List returned by Hibernate will contain an array of objects. Each array contains the selected properties, in the order they're listed in the query. So we'll get a list of two-element arrays; each array will contain an Integer followed by a String.

Example 9-11 shows how we can update main() in *QueryTest.java* to work with these arrays.

Example 9-11. Working with multiple, separate properties in query results

```
// Print IDs and titles of tracks that will fit in five minutes
List titles = tracksNoLongerThan(Time.valueOf("00:05:00"),
                                 session);
for (ListIterator iter = titles.listIterator() ;
    iter.hasNext() ; ) {
  Object[] aRow = (Object[])iter.next();
  Integer anID = (Integer)aRow[0];
  String aTitle = (String)aRow[1];
  System.out.println("Track: " + aTitle + " [ID=" + anID + ']');
}
```

Running **ant qtest** after these changes produces output like Example 9-12.

Example 9-12. Listing titles and IDs

```
qtest:
     [java] Track: Russian Trance [ID=0]
     [java] Track: Video Killed the Radio Star [ID=1]
     [java] Track: Test Tone 1 [ID=6]
     [java] Track: In a Manner of Speaking [ID=8]
     [java] Track: Gone [ID=10]
     [java] Track: Never Turn Your Back on Mother Earth [ID=11]
     [java] Track: Motherless Child [ID=12]
```

I hope that while looking at this example you thought "that's an awkward way to work with Track properties." If you didn't, compare Example 9-11 with lines 48–56 of Example 3-5. The latter is more concise and natural, and it prints even more information about the tracks. If you're extracting information about a mapped object, you're almost always better off taking full advantage of the mapping capability to extract an actual instance of the object, so you can work with its properties with the full expressive and type-safe capabilities of Java.

Was this some sort of cruel joke?

So why did I show it at all? Well, there are situations where retrieving multiple values in an HQL query can make sense: you might want just one property from each of a couple of mapped classes, for example. Or you might want to return a group of related classes by listing the class names in the select clause. For such cases it's worth knowing this technique. There may also be significant performance benefits if your mapped object has dozens of large (or non-lazily associated) properties, and you're only interested in one or two.

There is another surprising trick you can use to impose a good object structure even when you're building reports that select a bunch of properties from disparate mapped objects. HQL lets you construct and return an arbitrary object within your select clause. So you could create an ad-hoc reporting class whose properties reflect the values needed by your report, and return instances of this class in the query instead of cryptic Object arrays. If we'd defined a TrackSummary class with id and title properties and an appropriate constructor, our query could have used:

```
select new TrackSummary(track.id, track.title)
```

instead of:

```
select track.id, track.title
```

and we wouldn't have needed any of the array manipulation in the code that works with the results. (Again, in this case, it would still have made more sense to simply return the entire Track, but this is useful when you're working with properties from multiple objects or even synthetic results like aggregate functions, as demonstrated below.)

Sorting

It should come as no surprise that you can use a SQL-style "order by" clause to control the order in which your output appears. I've alluded to this several times in earlier chapters, and it works just like you'd expect. You can use any property of the objects being returned to establish the sort order, and you can list multiple properties to establish sub-sorts within results for which the first property values are the same.

How do I do that?

Sorting is very simple: you list the values that you want to use to sort the results. As usual, where SQL uses columns, HQL uses properties. For Example 9-13, let's update the query in Example 9-10 so that it displays the results in reverse alphabetical order.

Example 9-13. Addition to *Track.hbm.xml* that sorts the results backwards by title

```
<query name="com.oreilly.hh.tracksNoLongerThan">
  <![CDATA[
    select track.id, track.title from com.oreilly.hh.Track as track
    where track.playTime <= :length
    order by track.title desc
  ]]>
</query>
```

As in SQL, you specify an ascending sort using "asc" and a descending sort with "desc".

The output from running this is as you'd expect (Example 9-14).

Example 9-14. Titles and IDs in reverse alphabetical order

```
% ant qtest
Buildfile: build.xml

prepare:
     [copy] Copying 1 file to /Users/jim/Documents/Work/OReilly/Hibernate/
Examples/ch09/classes

compile:

qtest:
     [java] Track: Video Killed the Radio Star [ID=1]
     [java] Track: Test Tone 1 [ID=6]
     [java] Track: Russian Trance [ID=0]
     [java] Track: Never Turn Your Back on Mother Earth [ID=11]
     [java] Track: Motherless Child [ID=12]
     [java] Track: In a Manner of Speaking [ID=8]
     [java] Track: Gone [ID=10]
```

Working with Aggregate Values

Especially when writing reports, you'll often want summary information from the database: "How many? What's the average? The longest?" HQL can help with this, by offering aggregate functions like those in SQL. In HQL, of course, these functions apply to the properties of persistent classes.

How do I do that?

Let's try some of this in our query test framework. First, add the query in Example 9-15 after the existing query in *Track.hbm.xml*.

Example 9-15. A query collecting aggregate information about tracks

```
<query name="com.oreilly.hh.trackSummary">
  <![CDATA[
      select count(*), min(track.playTime), max(track.playTime)
      from com.oreilly.hh.Track as track
    ]]>
</query>
```

I was tempted to try asking for the average playing time as well, but unfortunately HSQLDB doesn't know how to calculate averages for non-numeric values, and this property is stored in a column of type date.

Next we need to write a method to run this query and display the results. Add the code in Example 9-16 to *QueryTest.java*, after the tracksNoLongerThan() method.

Example 9-16. A method to run the trackSummary query

```
/**
 * Print summary information about all tracks.
 *
 * @param session the Hibernate session that can retrieve data.
 * @throws HibernateException if there is a problem.
**/
public static void printTrackSummary(Session session)
    throws HibernateException
{
    Query query = session.getNamedQuery("com.oreilly.hh.trackSummary");
    Object[] results = (Object[])query.uniqueResult();
    System.out.println("Summary information:");
    System.out.println("      Total tracks: " + results[0]);
    System.out.println("    Shortest track: " + results[1]);
    System.out.println("     Longest track: " + results[2]);
}
```

Since we're only using aggregate functions in the query, we know we'll only get one row of results back. This is another opportunity to use the uniqueResult() convenience method offered by the Query interface. It saves us the trouble of getting back a list and extracting the first element. As discussed in the "Selecting Properties and Pieces" section above, since we've asked for multiple distinct values, that result will be an Object array, whose elements are the values we requested in the same order we put them in the query.

We also need to add a line to main() to call this method. We can put it after the end of the loop in which we print details about selected tracks, as shown in Example 9-17.

Example 9-17. Addition to main() in *QueryTest.java* to display the new summary information

```
...
      System.out.println("Track: " + aTitle + " [ID=" + anID + ']');
   }
   printTrackSummary(session);
} finally {
   // No matter what, close the session
...
```

With these additions, we get new output when running **ant qtest** (Example 9-18).

Example 9-18. The summary output

```
...
qtest:
      [java] Track: Video Killed the Radio Star [ID=1]
      [java] Track: Test Tone 1 [ID=6]
      [java] Track: Russian Trance [ID=0]
      [java] Track: Never Turn Your Back on Mother Earth [ID=11]
      [java] Track: Motherless Child [ID=12]
      [java] Track: In a Manner of Speaking [ID=8]
      [java] Track: Gone [ID=10]
      [java] Summary information:
      [java]         Total tracks: 13
      [java]       Shortest track: 00:00:10
      [java]        Longest track: 00:07:39
```

That was pretty easy. Let's try something trickier—pulling information from joined tables. Tracks have a collection of artists associated with them. Suppose we want to get summary information about the tracks associated with a particular artist, rather than for all tracks. Example 9-19 shows what we'd add to the query.

Example 9-19. Summarizing tracks associated with an artist

```
<query name="com.oreilly.hh.trackSummary">
  <![CDATA[
     select count(*), min(track.playTime), max(track.playTime)
     from com.oreilly.hh.Track as track
     where :artist in elements(track.artists)
  ]]>
</query>
```

We've added a where clause to narrow down the tracks we want to see, using a named parameter, artist. HQL provides another use for the in operator. While you can use it in the normal SQL sense to give a list of possible values for a property, you can also do what we've done here. This statement tells Hibernate we are interested in tracks whose artists collection contains a specified value. To call this version of the query, beef up printTrackSummary() a little, as shown in Example 9-20.

Example 9-20. Enhancing printTrackSummary() to work with a specific artist

```
/**
 * Print summary information about tracks associated with an artist.
 *
 * @param artist the artist in whose tracks we're interested
 * @param session the Hibernate session that can retrieve data.
 * @throws HibernateException if there is a problem.
 **/
public static void printTrackSummary(Artist artist, Session session)
    throws HibernateException
{
    Query query = session.getNamedQuery("com.oreilly.hh.trackSummary");
    query.setParameter("artist", artist);
    Object[] results = (Object[])query.uniqueResult();
    System.out.println("Summary of tracks by " + artist.getName() + ':');
    System.out.println("       Total tracks: " + results[0]);
    System.out.println("      Shortest track: " + results[1]);
    System.out.println("       Longest track: " + results[2]);
}
```

Wasn't much to that, was there? Finally, the line that calls this method needs another parameter to specify an artist. Use the handy getArtist() method in *CreateTest.java* once again. Change the method call in *QueryTest.java*'s main() method to look like it does in Example 9-21.

Example 9-21. Calling the enhanced printTrackSummary()

```
...
        System.out.println("Track: " + aTitle + " [ID=" + anID + ']');
    }
    printTrackSummary(CreateTest.getArtist("Samuel Barber",
                                    false, session), session);
```

Example 9-21. *Calling the enhanced printTrackSummary() (continued)*

```
} finally {
    // No matter what, close the session
...
```

Now when you run **ant qtest** you'll see information that looks like Example 9-22.

Example 9-22. *Running the summary query for tracks by Samuel Barber*

```
qtest:
    [java] Track: Video Killed the Radio Star [ID=1]
    [java] Track: Test Tone 1 [ID=6]
    [java] Track: Russian Trance [ID=0]
    [java] Track: Never Turn Your Back on Mother Earth [ID=11]
    [java] Track: Motherless Child [ID=12]
    [java] Track: In a Manner of Speaking [ID=8]
    [java] Track: Gone [ID=10]
    [java] Summary of tracks by Samuel Barber:
    [java]          Total tracks: 2
    [java]        Shortest track: 00:06:35
    [java]         Longest track: 00:07:39
```

What just happened?

This took so little effort that it's worth taking a minute to appreciate how much Hibernate actually did for us. The getArtist() method we called returned the Artist instance corresponding to Samuel Barber. We were able to pass this entire object as a named parameter to our HQL query, and Hibernate knows enough about how to put together join queries using the Artist's id property and the TRACK_ARTISTS table to implement the complicated condition we expressed so concisely in Example 9-19.

Just try doing something like that with vanilla SQL!

The results we got reflect the two remixes of "Adagio for Strings" in the sample data. They don't show up in the detailed track list because they're both longer than five minutes.

Writing Native SQL Queries

Given the power and convenience of HQL, and the way it dovetails so naturally with the objects in your Java code, why wouldn't you want to use it? Well, there might be some special feature supported by the native SQL dialect of your project's database that HQL can't exploit. If you're willing to accept the fact that using this feature will make it harder to change databases in the future, Hibernate will let you write queries in that native dialect while still helping you write expressions in terms of properties and translate the results to objects. (If you didn't want this help, you could just use a raw JDBC connection to run a plain SQL query, of course.)

Another circumstance in which it might be nice to meet your database halfway is if you're in the process of migrating an existing JDBC-based project to Hibernate, and you want to take small steps rather than thoroughly rewriting each query right away.

How do I do that?

If you're embedding your query text inside your Java source code, you use the Session method createSQLQuery() instead of Example 3-8's createQuery(). Of course, you know better than to code like that, so I won't even show you an example. The better approach is to put the query in a mapping document like Example 3-9. The difference is that you use a sql-query tag rather than the query tag we've seen up until now. You also need to tell Hibernate the mapped class you want to return, and the alias that you're using to refer to it (and its properties) in the query.

As a somewhat contrived example, suppose we want to know all the tracks that end exactly halfway through the last minute they're playing (in other words, the time display on the jukebox would be *h*:*mm*:30). An easy way to do that would be to take advantage of HSQLDB's built-in SECOND function, which gives you the seconds part of a Time value. Since HQL doesn't know about functions that are specific to HSQLDB's SQL dialect, this will push us into the realm of a native SQL query. Example 9-23 shows what it would look like; add this after the HQL queries in *Track.hbm.xml*.

Example 9-23. Embedding a native SQL dialect query in a Hibernate mapping

```
<sql-query name="com.oreilly.hh.tracksEndingAt">
  <return alias="track" class="com.oreilly.hh.Track"/>
  <![CDATA[
      select {track.*}
      from TRACK as {track}
      where SECOND({track}.PLAYTIME) = :seconds
  ]]>
</sql-query>
```

The return tag tells Hibernate we're going to be using the alias track in our query to refer to a Track object. That allows us to use the shorthand {track.*} in the query body to refer to all the columns from the TRACK table we need in order to create a Track instance. (Notice that everywhere we use the alias in the query body we need to enclose it in curly braces. This gets us "out of" the native SQL environment so we can express things in terms of Hibernate-mapped classes and properties.)

The where clause in the query uses the HSQLDB SECOND function to narrow our results to include only tracks whose length has a specified number in the seconds part. Happily, even though we're building a native SQL query, we can still make use of Hibernate's nice named query parameters. In this case we're passing in a value named "seconds" to control the query. (You don't use curly braces to tell Hibernate you're using a named parameter even in an SQL query; its parser is smart enough to figure this out.)

The code that uses this mapped SQL query is no different than our previous examples using HQL queries. The getNamedQuery() method is used to load both kinds, and they both implement the Query interface. So our Java method invoking this query should look familiar. Add the code in Example 9-24 after the printTrackSummary() method in *QueryTest.java*.

Example 9-24. Calling a native SQL mapped query

```
/**
 * Print tracks that end some number of seconds into their final minute.
 *
 * @param seconds, the number of seconds at which we want tracks to end.
 * @param session the Hibernate session that can retrieve data.
 * @throws HibernateException if there is a problem.
 **/
public static void printTracksEndingAt(int seconds, Session session)
    throws HibernateException
{
    Query query = session.getNamedQuery("com.oreilly.hh.tracksEndingAt");
    query.setInteger("seconds", seconds);
    List results = query.list();
    for (ListIterator iter = results.listIterator() ; iter.hasNext() ; ) {
        Track aTrack = (Track)iter.next();
        System.out.println("Track: " + aTrack.getTitle() +
                           ", length=" + aTrack.getPlayTime());
    }
}
```

Finally, add some lines to main() that call this method. Example 9-25 shows them added after the invocation of printTrackSummary().

Example 9-25. Calling printTracksEndingAt() to display tracks ending at a half minute

```
...
    printTrackSummary(CreateTest.getArtist("Samuel Barber",
                                           false, session), session);
    System.out.println("Tracks ending halfway through final minute:");
    printTracksEndingAt(30, session);
} finally {
    // No matter what, close the session
...
```

These changes produce the additional output shown in Example 9-26 when **ant qtest** is run.

Example 9-26. Sample output from the native SQL query

```
qtest:
    [java] Track: Video Killed the Radio Star [ID=1]
    ...
    [java] Summary of tracks by Samuel Barber:
    [java]        Total tracks: 2
    [java]      Shortest track: 00:06:35
    [java]       Longest track: 00:07:39
    [java] Tracks ending halfway through final minute:
    [java] Track: Russian Trance, length=00:03:30
```

There's a lot more tedium and attention to detail required in using a native SQL query than an HQL query (especially when your query starts getting complex or referring to multiple tables), but it's nice to know that it is possible on the rare occasions where you really need one.

What about...

...Well, lots of things? You undoubtedly suspect this chapter barely scratches the surface of what you can do with HQL. That's definitely true. When you start combining some of these capabilities, and working with collections, associations, and powerful expressions, you can achieve some remarkable things. We can't possibly cover them all in this introduction, so you'll want to take a close look at the HQL section and examples in the Hibernate reference documentation, and do some experimentation on your own.

When you look through the Hibernate Query Language chapter in the reference documentation, be sure to look at the interesting things you can use in expressions, especially as they apply to collections. Don't miss the way you can use array bracket notation to select elements of indexed collections—you can even put arithmetic expressions inside the brackets.

This isn't your father's SQL...

The "Tips and Tricks" section that follows their longer examples gives some useful advice about working efficiently in different database environments, and using a variety of Hibernate interfaces to achieve useful results in ways you might not think of, especially if you're coming from a SQL background.

Hopefully, this discussion has helped you get a grounding in the basics, and it will serve as a starting point and anchor for the explorations on which you will embark!

Hibernate Types

Hibernate makes a fundamental distinction between two different kinds of data in terms of how they relate to the persistence service: *entities* and *values*.

An entity is something with its own independent existence, regardless of whether it's currently reachable by any object within a Java virtual machine. Entities can be retrieved from the database through queries, and they must be explicitly saved and deleted by the application. (If cascading relationships have been set up, the act of saving or deleting a parent entity can also save or delete its children, but this is still explicit at the level of the parent.)

Values are stored only as part of the persistent state of an entity. They have no independent existence. They might be primitives, collections, enumerations, and custom user types. Since they are entirely subordinated to the entity in which they exist, they cannot be independently versioned, nor can they be shared by more than one entity or collection.

Notice that a particular Java object might be either an entity or a value— the difference is in how it is designed and presented to the persistence service. Primitive Java types are always values.

Basic Types

Hibernate's basic types fall into a number of groupings:

Simple numeric and Boolean types
> These correspond to the primitive Java types that represent numbers, characters and Boolean values, or their wrapper classes. They get mapped to appropriate SQL column types (based on the SQL dialect in use). They are: boolean, byte, character, double, float, integer, long,

short, true_false, and yes_no. The last two are alternate ways to represent a Boolean value within the database; true_false uses the values "T" and "F", while yes_no uses "Y" and "N".

String type

The Hibernate type string maps from java.lang.String to the appropriate string column type for the SQL dialect (usually VARCHAR, but in Oracle VARCHAR2 is used).

Time types

Hibernate uses date, time, and timestamp to map from java.util.Date (and subclasses) to appropriate SQL types (e.g., DATE, TIME, TIMESTAMP).

Arbitrary precision numeric

The Hibernate type big_decimal provides a mapping between java.math.BigDecimal to the appropriate SQL type (usually NUMERIC, but Oracle uses NUMBER).

Localization values

The types locale, timezone, and currency are stored as strings (VARCHAR or VARCHAR2 as noted above), and mapped to the Locale, TimeZone, and Currency classes in the java.util package. Locale and Currency are stored using their ISO codes, while TimeZone is stored using its ID property.

Class names

The type class maps instances of java.lang.Class using their fully qualified names, stored in a string column (VARCHAR, or VARCHAR2 in Oracle).

Byte arrays

The type binary stores byte arrays in an appropriate SQL binary type.

Any serializable object

The type serializable can be used to map any serializable Java object into a SQL binary column. This is the fallback type used when attempting to persist an object that doesn't have a more specific appropriate mapping (and does not implement PersistentEnum; see the next section).

JDBC large objects

The types blob and clob provide mappings for the Blob and Clob classes in the java.sql package. Note that there are rather severe restrictions on using these classes. Driver support is rather inconsistent in the first place, and they can't be reused past a single transaction.

Persistent Enumerated Types

Hibernate provides a mechanism to help map the common Java type-safe enumeration pattern to a database column. Unfortunately, the approach taken requires your enumerations to have an integer representation to store in the database, forcing them back to the lowest common denominator semantics of the enum type in the C language. I hope that a richer, string-based storage mechanism will eventually be supported, to dovetail nicely with the built-in support for this idiom that is coming in Tiger (Java Version 1.5). Storing enumerations as strings would also make them more readable to users of the raw database, a form of self-documenting storage.

To work with the current Hibernate implementation, your enumeration classes need only implement the net.sf.hibernate.PersistentEnum interface, and its fromInt() and toInt() methods. This is demonstrated in Chapter 6.

Custom Value Types

In addition to mapping your objects as entities, you can also create classes that are mapped to the database as values within other entities, without their own independent existence. This can be as simple as changing the way an existing type is mapped (because you want to use a different column type or representation), or as complex as splitting a value across multiple columns.

Although you can do this on a case-by-case basis within your mapping documents, the principle of avoiding repeated code argues for encapsulating types you use in more than one place into an actual reusable class. Your class will implement either net.sf.hibernate.UserType or net.sf. hibernate.CompositeUserType. This technique is illustrated in Chapter 7.

"Any" Type Mappings

This final kind of mapping is very much a free-for-all. Essentially, it allows you to map references to any of your other mapped entities interchangeably. This is done by providing two columns, one which contains the name of the table to which each reference is being made, and another which provides the ID within that table of the specific entity of interest.

You can't maintain any sort of foreign key constraints in such a loose relationship. It's rare to need this kind of mapping at all. One situation in which you might find it useful is if you want to maintain an audit log that can contain actual objects. The reference manual also mentions web application session data as another potential use, but that seems unlikely in a well-structured application.

All Types

The following table shows each of the type classes in the net.sf. hibernate.types package, along with the type name you would use for it in a mapping document, the SQL type used in columns storing mapped values, and any relevant comments about its purpose. In many cases, more detailed discussion can be found earlier. To save space, the "Type" which appears at the end of each class name has been removed, except in the case of the Type interface implemented by all the others.

Type class	Type name	SQL type	Notes
Abstract-Component	N/A	N/A	Abstract ancestor of Component, DynaBean, and Object types
Abstract	N/A	N/A	Abstract skeleton used by the built-in types
Array	N/A	N/A	Maps a Java array as a Persistent-Collection
Association	N/A	N/A	Interface used by all associations between entities
Bag	N/A	N/A	Maps collections with bag semantics
BigDecimal	big_decimal	NUMERIC	In Oracle, SQL type is NUMBER
Binary	binary	VARBINARY	Basic type for byte arrays
Blob	blob	BLOB	Not all drivers support this
Boolean	boolean	BIT	A basic type
Byte	byte	TINYINT	A basic type
CalendarDate	calendar_date	DATE	A basic type
Calendar	calendar	TIMESTAMP	A basic type
CharBoolean	N/A	CHAR	Abstract skeleton used to implement yes_no and true_false types
Character	character	CHAR	A basic and primitive type
Class	class	VARCHAR or VARCHAR2	Basic type that stores a class' name
Clob	clob	CLOB	Not all drivers support this

Type class	Type name	SQL type	Notes
Component	N/A	N/A	Maps the properties of a contained value class on to a group of columns
Composite-Custom	N/A	N/A	Adapts CompositeUserType implementations to the Type interface
Currency	currency	VARCHAR or VARCHAR2	Stores ISO code for a currency
Custom	N/A	N/A	Adapts UserType implementations to the Type interface
Date	date	DATE	A basic type
Discriminator	N/A	N/A	Marker interface for types that can be used for discriminator properties (to select the right mapped subclass)
Double	double	DOUBLE	A basic and primitive type
DynaBean	N/A	N/A	Maps Jakarta Commons DynaBeans
Entity	N/A	N/A	Represents a reference to another entity
Float	float	FLOAT	A basic and primitive type
IdentifierBag	N/A	N/A	Supports experimental idbag, mapping a Collection with bag semantics
Identifier	N/A	N/A	Marker interface for types that store identifiers of entities
Immutable	N/A	N/A	Abstract superclass for immutable types; extends NullableType
Integer	integer	INTEGER	A basic and primitive type
List	N/A	N/A	Maps a Java List
Literal	N/A	N/A	Marker interface for types that store SQL literals
Locale	locale	VARCHAR or VARCHAR2	Stores ISO code for a locale
Long	long	LONG	A basic and primitive type
ManyToOne	N/A	N/A	An association between entities
Map	N/A	N/A	Maps a Java Map
Mutable	N/A	N/A	Abstract superclass for mutable types
Nullable	N/A	N/A	Abstract superclass for simple, one column types that can be null
Object	N/A	N/A	Handles "any" type mappings
OneToOne	N/A	N/A	An association between entities
Persistent-Collection	N/A	N/A	Supports persistence of collections and arrays
PersistentEnum	N/A	N/A	Maps persistent enumerations
Primitive	N/A	N/A	Abstract skeleton for mapping primitive Java types; extends ImmutableType

Type class	Type name	SQL type	Notes
Serializable	serial-izable	Binary, depends on SQL dialect	Catch-all mapping for serializable classes with no better alternative
Set	N/A	N/A	Maps a Java Set
Short	short	SMALLINT	A basic and primitive type
SortedMap	N/A	N/A	Sorted extension of MapType
SortedSet	N/A	N/A	Sorted extension of SetType
String	string	VARCHAR or VARCHAR2	A basic and primitive type
Time	time	TIME	A basic type
TimeZone	timezone	VARCHAR or VARCHAR2	Stores time zone ID
Timestamp	timestamp	TIMESTAMP	A basic type
TrueFalse	true_false	CHAR	Stores Booleans as "T" or "F"
Type	N/A	N/A	Superinterface of all these types
Version	N/A	N/A	Extends Type for version stamping
YesNo	yes_no	CHAR	Stores Booleans as "Y" or "N"

There is also a TypeFactory class which provides assistance in building the right Type implementation for a given need, such as when parsing a type name in a mapping document. Reading its source is interesting.

Standard Criteria

The Expression Factory

Hibernate provides the class net.sf.hibernate.expression.Expression as a factory for creating the Criterion instances you use to set up criteria queries. Expression defines a bunch of static methods you can invoke to conveniently create each of the standard Criterion implementations available in Hibernate, using parameters you supply. These criteria are used to determine which persistent objects from the database are included in the results of your query. Here is a summary of the available options.

Method	Parameters	Purpose
allEq	Map properties	A shortcut for requiring several properties to have particular values. The keys of the supplied map are the names of the properties you want to constrain, while the values in the map are the target values each property must equal if an entity is to be included in the query results. The returned Criterion ensures that each named property has the corresponding value.
and	Criterion lhs, Criterion rhs	Builds a compound Criterion that requires both halves to be met in order for the whole to succeed.
between	String property, Object low, Object high	Requires the value of the named property to fall between the values of low and high.
conjunction	None	Creates a Conjunction object which can be used to build an "and" criterion with as many pieces as you need. Simply call its add() method with each of the Criterion instances you want to check. The conjunction will be true if and only if all its component criteria are true. This is more convenient than building a tree of and() criteria "by hand." The add() method of the Criteria interface acts as though it contains a Conjunction.

Method	Parameters	Purpose
disjunction	None	Creates a `Disjunction` object that can be used to build an "or" criterion with as many pieces as you need. Simply call its `add()` method with each of the `Criterion` instances you want to check. The disjunction will be true if any of its component criteria are true. This is more convenient than building a tree of `or()` criteria "by hand." See Example 8-10.
eq	`String property, Object value`	Requires the named property to have the specified value.
eqProperty	`String property1, String property2`	Requires the two named properties to have the same value.
ge	`String property, Object value`	Requires the named property to be greater than or equal to the specified value.
gt	`String property, Object value`	Requires the named property to be greater than the specified value.
ilike	`String property, String value`	A case-insensitive "like" operator. See `like`, below.
ilike	`String property, String value, MatchMode mode`	A case-insensitive "like" operator for people who don't want to mess with "like" syntax and just want to match a substring. `MatchMode` is a type-safe enumeration with values `START`, `END`, `ANYWHERE`, and `EXACT`. This method simply adjusts the syntax of `value` to reflect the kind of matching specified by `mode`, then calls the two-parameter `ilike()`.
in	`String property, Collection values`	A shortcut for allowing the named property to have any of the values contained in the collection. This is more convenient than building up a `disjunction()` of `eq()` criteria "by hand."
in	`String property, Object[] values`	A shortcut for allowing the named property to have any of the values contained in the array. This is more convenient than building up a `disjunction()` of `eq()` criteria "by hand."
isNotNull	`String property`	Requires the named property to have a value other than `null`.
isNull	`String property`	Requires the named property to be `null`.
le	`String property, Object value`	Requires the named property to be less than or equal to the specified value. See Example 8-3.
leProperty	`String property1, String property2`	Requires the first named property to be less than or equal to the second.
like	`String property, String value`	Requires the named property to be "like" the specified value (in the sense of the SQL `like` operator, which allows simple pattern matching). See Example 8-8 and Example 8-13.

Method	Parameters	Purpose
like	String property, String value, MatchMode mode	A "like" operator for people who don't want to mess with "like" syntax and just want to match a substring. MatchMode is a type-safe enumeration with values START, END, ANYWHERE, and EXACT. This method simply adjusts the syntax of value to reflect the kind of matching specified by mode, then calls the two-parameter like().
lt	String property, Object value	Requires the named property to be less than the specified value.
ltProperty	String property1, String property2	Requires the first named property to be less than the second.
not	Criterion value	Negates the supplied Criterion (if it matched, this one fails, and vice versa).
or	Criterion lhs, Criterion rhs	Builds a compound Criterion that succeeds if either of its halves matches.
sql	String sql	Apply a constraint expressed in the native SQL dialect of the underlying database system. This can be very powerful, but be aware it might lead to loss of portability.
sql	String sql, Object[] values, Type[] types	Apply a constraint expressed in the native SQL of the underlying database, with the supplied JDBC parameters. This can be very powerful, but be aware it might lead to loss of portability.
sql	String sql, Object value, Type type	Apply a constraint expressed in the native SQL of the underlying database, with the supplied JDBC parameters. This can be very powerful, but be aware it might lead to loss of portability.

When specifying query text for the sql() methods, any occurrences of the string "{alias}" within the query will be replaced by the actual alias of the table on which the query is being performed.

Many of these methods accept Criterion instances as arguments, allowing you to build compound criteria trees of as much complexity as you need. conjunction() and disjunction() return objects that make it even easier to add criteria, by returning objects with add() methods you can call as many times as you'd like to add criteria. If your query gets sufficiently complex, however, it might be easier to express and understand in HQL. There are also some kinds of queries that are not yet supported by this API, so you may not always be able to avoid HQL even if you want to.

Despite these caveats, many of the kinds of bread-and-butter queries that come up all the time in application development are expressed very naturally and easily in this API, leading to readable and compact Java code.

Hibernate SQL Dialects

Getting Fluent in the Local SQL

Hibernate ships with detailed support for many commercial and free relational databases. While most features will work properly without doing so, it's important to set the `hibernate.dialect` configuration property to the right subclass of `net.sf.hibernate.dialect.Dialect`, especially if you want to use features like `native` or `sequence` primary key generation or session locking. Choosing a dialect is also a very convenient way of setting up a whole raft of Hibernate configuration parameters you'd otherwise have to deal with individually.

Database system	Appropriate hibernate.dialect setting
DB2	net.sf.hibernate.dialect.DB2Dialect
FrontBase	net.sf.hibernate.dialect.FrontbaseDialect
HSQLDB	net.sf.hibernate.dialect.HSQLDialect
Informix	net.sf.hibernate.dialect.InformixDialect
Ingres	net.sf.hibernate.dialect.IngresDialect
Interbase	net.sf.hibernate.dialect.InterbaseDialect
Mckoi SQL	net.sf.hibernate.dialect.MckoiDialect
Microsoft SQL Server	net.sf.hibernate.dialect.SQLServerDialect
MySQL	net.sf.hibernate.dialect.MySQLDialect
Oracle (any version)	net.sf.hibernate.dialect.OracleDialect
Oracle 9 (specifically)	net.sf.hibernate.dialect.Oracle9Dialect
Pointbase	net.sf.hibernate.dialect.PointbaseDialect
PostgreSQL	net.sf.hibernate.dialect.PostgreSQLDialect
Progress	net.sf.hibernate.dialect.ProgressDialect
SAP DB	net.sf.hibernate.dialect.SAPDBDialect
Sybase	net.sf.hibernate.dialect.SybaseDialect
Sybase Anywhere	net.sf.hibernate.dialect.SybaseAnywhereDialect

If you don't see your target database here, check whether support has been added to the latest Hibernate release. The dialects are listed in the "SQL Dialects" section of the Hibernate reference documentation. If that doesn't pan out, see if you can find a third-party effort to support the database, or consider starting your own!

Index

We'd like to hear your suggestions for improving our indexes. Send email to *index@oreilly.com*.

About the Author

James Elliott is a senior software engineer at Berbee, with over 15 years of professional experience as a systems developer. A decade before that career, he cultivated his involvement and fascination with computers, and started designing with objects well before his work environments made it convenient. He has a passion for building high-quality tools and frameworks to simplify the tasks of other developers, and loves how using Java effectively can help in that effort. After a globe-trotting childhood, Jim earned his bachelor's degree in computer science at Rensselaer Polytechnic in upstate New York and his master's at the University of Wisconsin–Madison, with some interesting stints at Bell Laboratories (in Murray Hill, birthplace of C and Unix). Although he succumbed to the allure of the real world shortly after completing his Ph.D. qualifying exams, he was happy to find interesting work in Madison, where he lives with his partner Joe Buberger and two challenging cats.

Colophon

Our look is the result of reader comments, our own experimentation, and feedback from distribution channels. Distinctive covers complement our distinctive approach to technical topics, breathing personality and life into potentially dry subjects.

The *Developer's Notebook* series is modeled on the tradition of laboratory notebooks. Laboratory notebooks are an invaluable tool for researchers and their successors.

The purpose of a laboratory notebook is to facilitate the recording of data and conclusions as the work is being conducted, creating a faithful and immediate history. The notebook begins with a title page that includes the owner's name and the subject of research. The pages of the notebook should be numbered and prefaced with a table of contents. Entries must be clear, easy to read, and accurately dated; they should use simple, direct language to indicate the name of the experiment and the steps taken. Calculations are written out carefully and relevant thoughts and ideas recorded. Each experiment is introduced and summarized as it is added to the notebook. The goal is to produce comprehensive, clearly organized notes that can be used as a reference. Careful documentation creates a valuable record and provides a practical guide for future developers.

Colleen Gorman was the production editor and Marlowe Shaeffer was the proofreader for *Hibernate: A Developer's Notebook*. Mary Agner and Jamie Peppard provided production support. Claire Cloutier provided quality control. Tom Dinse wrote the index.

Edie Freedman designed the cover of this book. Emma Colby produced the cover layout with QuarkXPress 4.1 using the Officina Sans and JuniorHandwriting fonts.

Edie Freedman and David Futato designed the interior layout. This book was converted by Julie Hawks to FrameMaker 5.5.6 with a format conversion tool created by Erik Ray, Jason McIntosh, Neil Walls, and Mike Sierra that uses Perl and XML technologies. The text font is Adobe Boton; the heading font is ITC Officina Sans; the code font is LucasFont's TheSans Mono Condensed, and the handwriting font is a modified version of JRHand made by Tepid Monkey Fonts and modified by O'Reilly. The illustrations that appear in the book were produced by Robert Romano and Jessamyn Read using Macromedia FreeHand 9 and Adobe Photoshop 6. This colophon was written by Colleen Gorman.

Lightning Source UK Ltd.
Milton Keynes UK
UKHW031822191222
414174UK00009B/683